IRISH VOICES, IRISH LIVES

B E N   L A N D E R

BRANDON

First published in 1997 by
Brandon Book Publishers Ltd,
Dingle, Co. Kerry, Ireland

© Ben Lander 1997

British Library Cataloguing in Publication Data
is available for this book.

ISBN 0 86322 230 7

Typeset by Brandon
Cover design by Peter Staunton, Design Gang, Tralee
Printed by Colour Books Ltd, Dublin

IRISH VOICES: IRISH LIVES

For Clare

Contents

Foreword

The following twelve interviews are an attempt to explore the Ireland of today. My original idea was to write a travel book, and although the form did not turn out as I had first planned, I still see it as such.

As a foreigner, Irish society seems very complex and diverse to me. To find my way through this complexity and diversity, I needed help and guidance, and I got it in abundance, not only from the twelve people who are included in this book, but also from all the other people that I have interviewed during my 'journey'. They have all played their parts in forming this work, and I would like to thank them for sharing their time, their experiences, thoughts and ideas with me.

I am of course responsible for the choice of interviews and topics. I have not tried to give a complete picture of Ireland. This is 'my' portrait of 'my' Ireland, and focuses on the questions that I find especially burning and interesting in this intense time of transition and change which many areas of Irish society are experiencing. My hope is that this book will contribute to a picture of Ireland which shows it not as a stereotype but as a living, multifaceted society. I invite the reader to accompany me and my fellow travellers on our little odyssey through this most beautiful and intriguing island.

Ben Lander
Marshallstown, County Meath
February 1997

People interviewed

Seamus Hogan lives in County Cork where he breeds free-range pigs. He is show-secretary of the Irish Rare Breeds Society. He is also a poet and has published two collections of poetry.

Nell McDonagh lives in Navan with her family, where she works as a pre-school teacher for traveller children. She is also a community activist working for travellers' rights, and is a member of the Irish Traveller Movement and the Traveller Women's Forum.

Pat Buckley is a Catholic priest living in Larne, County Antrim. Well known for his liberal views, he has been strongly critical of the Church hierarchy.

Jim McAllister was elected to the Northern Ireland Assembly in 1992 and is now a Sinn Féin councillor in the town of Crossmaglen, County Armagh, which lies on the border between Northern Ireland and the Republic.

Billy Hutchinson lives in Belfast and is an executive member of the Progressive Unionist Party. He was involved in brokering the Loyalist ceasefire in 1994 and is at present a delegate to the Northern Ireland Forum.

Seán Ó Siadhail, originally from Derry, lives in County Meath with his Irish-speaking family. A teacher by profession, he is also a writer in Irish, with several novels and short story collections published.

Noreen Byrne, chairperson of the National Women's Council of

Ireland, has been campaigning for women's rights for the last twenty years. She is the founder of Parents Alone, and has written a book about abortion, *Choices: For Women With Crisis Pregnancies*.

Gráinne Daly is an up-and-coming matchmaker from County Clare, where she and her father fight against the depopulation of the countryside by bringing couples together.

Pat Tierney was a busker of poetry on Grafton Street, Dublin, and author of the outspoken autobiography, *The Moon On My Back*. He had a long experience of fighting against social issues and injustices. This interview was made in the autumn of 1995. Pat has since taken his own life.

Eunice McCarthy, a native of Tralee, County Kerry, is professor of Social Psychology in the Department of Psychology, University College Dublin. She is particularly interested in the links between Celtic culture and contemporary experience.

Margaret Mac Curtain is a Dominican Sister and a noted historian. Here she asks: are the Irish a particularly spiritual people?

Maureen Hogan is a widow with five children, and a member of the Irish Countrywomen's Association. Though she is blind, she lives alone on her farm in County Tipperary. She is a natural force who carries on baking, despite all changes.

Seamus Hogan

I BOUGHT THE THREE first pigs in 1991. I was on the dole at the time. I had fifty quid and I borrowed fifty more. One of them, Hazel, died in three days. I didn't have any place of my own then (I lived in an old gate-lodge with no land), so I loaned them out to various neighbours to dig their gardens. They are fast diggers, and the gardens were soon done, but fortunately another man in the area, Charles Harold Barry, had a forest I could put them in.

I didn't know anything at all about pigs at that time, so to learn how to rear them I became their student. For example, when designing a hut for them I gave them a choice of three designs and then developed the hut they chose to live in. Basically, everything I know about them today I have learned directly from them. When it was time for the first litter to come, I didn't know about the nest pigs make to farrow in, and kept removing the debris as fast as the sow brought it into the hut. Result? When she farrowed, eight or nine bonhams rolled out of the hut during the night and died of exposure. If I had left the nest debris alone, they would not have been able to get out. It was an expensive lesson. If you don't do your homework with pigs, the teacher will die.

Small pigs especially are very sensitive to change in atmosphere, or diet, or even to ownership. I still have two of the original three that I bought. One is called Victoria, named after the woman I bought her from. I consequently had to call the other one Maeve, which is the name of a legendary Irish queen. You can never be too careful in this country. Without knowing it, you might upset some nationalistic feelings.

Then Damaris and I bought this monastery with fourteen acres. It was a big change. It meant that I didn't need to carry a hundredweight of barley on my back through the forest every day. When we moved in, it's two years ago now, the land was totally overgrown with briars. Everybody said we would need a Hymac to clean it out. I thought that would be an awful waste when I could feed the pigs on it. Also, a Hymac would have scared the pigs. They would have thought it was a dinosaur or something. The neighbour had a digger in his place last year and my boar hid in the bushes for two days! Besides that, it would have cost a fortune, and made noise and pollution into the bargain, so I forgot the machinery and stuck to the pigs. One year later they had cleaned out so much I could plough, and this summer there is beet, turnips, cabbage and potatoes growing where there was wilderness, and the pigs did the clearing free of charge. No. More than that, I sold the offspring at a profit.

Our pigs are part of the farm rotation system. On this farm we don't have a problem with animal muck or slurry. When we move the pigs from a field, that field is ploughed and planted without the need for any artificial fertilisers. In the animal kingdom, pig shit is a most valuable manure. You'd need to keep a columbarium to do better.

When we moved in, the fencing wasn't up to scratch and the odd pig got out. One morning I thought Lottie was slow coming out of her hut, but didn't worry too much about it as I had more animals to feed. Then our neighbour, Paddy Crowley, God rest him, drew into the yard and I sort of knew then where Lottie was, but at the same time I saw two magpies so I thought it can't be too bad.

'Good morning,' he says.

'A lovely morning,' I say. Waiting.

'Ahem... you are not missing a pig by any chance?' he says.

You have to remember that we were only here a short time, and the neighbouring farmers were expecting pigs to escape regularly and go ploughing up their crops or start chasing cars like dogs.

'Ah, yes, you mean Lottie?' I said.

'Now, I don't know her name, but there is a big black sow above in the yard.'

'Well, if you give me a second, I will get a bucket of meal and go up with you.'

He was genuinely nonplussed. He must have thought I was going to feed the pig there and then leave her.

'But... but what about a trailer and some men to load her?' he wondered.

'No problem. She'll walk down with me. Good for her anyway. She's a bit too fat.' She still is; look at her over there.

So we went, it's only a couple of hundred yards, and there was Mary Crowley with a shovel trying to keep Lottie out of their spuds. She asked, pale, if it was dangerous.

'No, she's a dote. Come on, Lottie, let's go now.' And with that Lottie trotted over to me, had a mouthful of grain and off we went, with Paddy and Mary staring.

Pigs are so intelligent that you can train them basic things in a week. You know, pigs can learn about 600 different sounds, or command words, double the amount of a Grœnendahl, which is said to be the most intelligent dog that exists... bar your own, I suppose.

My pigs spend a hundred per cent of their lives outside,

except for last winter when the weather was so bad that they didn't want to be out. For a time I had to have them in open housing, which means that they had access to daylight. Usually the only time they go inside is to the abbatoir. No matter how much or what you feed pigs, they will root if they can, and if they can't they go insane. They just love being outside, and that's where they belong. Sunburn is the only thing to keep an eye out for, but it isn't a problem as long as the wallows are replenished.

I'll tell you a story. I had a Saddleback boar, nicknamed Eumaois after the swineherd that guarded Odysseus's pigs while he was away on his important adventures. Eumaois was a great pig who consistently sired big litters, but the problem with today's consumer is that the very sight of fat puts him or her off. A purebred Saddleback will, at seventy kilos live weight, have a backfat measurement of fifteen to sixteen millimetres, whereas his indoor cousin, the white blue-eyed, will have eight to ten millimetres of backfat at an even heavier weight. So I had no choice but to get rid of Eumaois and buy a meatline boar from a specialist indoor breeder. For the first few days, I kept him inside while training him to get used to the electric fence. When I did let him out into the orchard, it was incredible. The pig was a year old and had never been in the open air. He very tenderly took a few steps – then froze! He had seen an apple tree! Meatline boars don't have a lot of hair, but if he had been an Irish greyhound, the hair would have stood on the back of his neck. For perhaps four or five minutes he was rooted to the spot. I suppose he was tearing back through generations of pigs trying to find a memory of a tree. Poor chap, but he is very happy now. A big smile on his face every day.

I don't cut my pigs' teeth or clip their tails or give them iron

14

injections. I don't need to. My pigs have plenty to occupy them and plenty of space to get away from each other when they are young and establishing a hierarchy within the litter. Nor do I castrate the males. In fact, the only time I touch them is to scratch them. They love to be scratched on their back. They are the happiest animals I have ever seen. They shine like porcelain, *lain de pork*. You can see from the bloom of their coats that they are healthy. A couple of months ago, Babble had fourteen bonhams – I rarely have less than twelve in a litter – under a beech tree close to the stream... You see the tree there at the other side of the pond? Pretty nice, isn't it? I read in the *Lancet* that women who suffer from post-natal depression are treated with a drug made out of placenta. Just to be sure with my pigs, I let the sows eat the dead thing that is always with the litter.

Thank God – and the way we breed and treat them – my pigs are rarely sick. At the beginning Maeve and Victoria failed to come out of the hut one morning, and I panicked and called Mrs Thornton. I told her the pigs were behaving in the most peculiar manner. When they were out they were mooching and didn't show any interest in their food, and looked at me as if it was the end of the world. Have you ever seen the eyes of a Saddleback? They are beautifully brown. So Mrs Thornton listened and said that they probably were in heat. She was right. That's one of the few times I have had any reason to contact the vet. Sometimes they might get a runny snout or a cough, but it passes. The common cold, I would imagine.

Do you know that with pedigree Saddlebacks you have to cut lumps out of their ears to mark them? Each lump represents a number. I don't like that mutilation. My theory is that pigs are a bit like bats. They use their ears to locate food in the ground. I believe they emit a sound, inaudible to humans, into the earth, and when it returns they discern by its frequency whether there's a stone or a spud, a trinket or a truffle. I am convinced that every time you cut a lump out of their ear their ability to survive in my type of set-up is diminished. I wrote to the pig association asking if there was some more humane alternative to it. I got a kind letter back saying they were going to look into the matter. In other words, they thought I was a complete fool.

It has been an unbelievable amount of work to create a market. Today I have an extensive private clientele, from our next-door neighbour to clients in Dublin. Apart from that, I also sell to the delicatessen On the Pig's Back in the English Market in Cork. I have also been selling to Twohig's Super Valu in Kanturk, and once I've tightened up the packaging, I'll be selling there again, and to O'Connell's in Buttevant. For ourselves, I cure and sometimes smoke bits of pork. I have to. After couscous and merguez, bacon and cabbage is my favourite dish. In fact, when Damaris and I first met, she wouldn't eat bacon because of the way pigs are usually reared. So part of our courtship was a promise from me to produce an ethically edible bacon and cabbage.

The secret of this meat is in the taste. It is extraordinary. As I said, I don't use any chemicals, other than to worm the pigs once. Of course the Five Freedoms, the five basic welfare requirements – freedom from malnutrition, freedom from thermal and physical discomfort, freedom from injury and disease, freedom from fear and stress, and freedom to express most normal socially acceptable patterns of behaviour – are my starting point, but on top of that, I don't wean until the piglets are eight weeks old, and as soon as the mother has been served, I return her to her family. Not Harry though, she is different. I think she hates bonhams.

I want a customer base that has a complete trust in this meat. I think it is a customer's right to be able to trust what he or she pays for to eat. As it is today, you too often risk your life when you stick something to eat into your mouth. Have you seen the fields in Ireland today? They are not green any more, they are f-ing blue from all the chemicals. No wonder the Atlantic is shifting colour.

Anybody that buys one of my chops can come and see how the production is done. If anybody in Dublin buys my meat, they can ring me and get an appointment and come to my place. That might only be for another period, though. It's already too much like an open farm. People seem to be very curious about Saddlebacks. Saddlebacks, like quite a few other domestic animals, are an endangered species, so if I'm not remembered for anything else, I'll probably be remembered as 'the fella with the black pigs'.

Yes, I have a few other aims with my meat. You know, thirty or forty years ago, when the farm labourers were looking for work, if they didn't see a ham hanging in the kitchen they expected a rough time. Either the house was mean, or poor. You can see yourself, we have no ham hanging, and it's not out of meanness. Wouldn't it be nice to have a Kanturk ham hanging in the middle of Ireland, instead of a Parma from Italy? Cooked meat, which is the literal translation of *charcuterie*, could, and hopefully with my help will, be developed in Ireland. Free-range pork is not readily available in Ireland today. In fact, most free-range pork that you buy in England isn't really free-range. The sows do spend their lives outside, but the bonhams are weaned at twenty-four days and go straight into the conventional units. I suppose it's a start. I'd love to think that the consumer would eventually realise that there is a limit to how far the farmer can go in producing assembly line food. I think most farmers have already passed that limit, not because they want to, but because advertising is such a strong force. No fat is allowed any more. They say you can't eat butter because it's too fat. Instead they want to feed you some readyspread that gives you cancer.

For some time I have been selling gilts to satellite farmers. Under contract, I have the right to use their name and address on the label when I sell the meat. I have the right to call to their farm at any time for a check, to take samples of the feed and of the meat, and if I find any forbidden products they are excluded from the group. The local grain merchant makes up a special ration without antibiotics and growth enhancers. The members of the group are not happy about the set-up: they are delighted. Try to organise a market yourself and you'll understand why. I have to have a market for their meat. I get the first choice of six out of every litter. Anything after that they can keep or sell to whoever they want. We are having a meeting soon to set up the prices for next year. It's a tough business. It's like the stock-market. In fact, a young female pig is even called a gilt before she becomes a sow.

My pigs are for making a small living. I like small scale. It gives me freedom. I can do a bit of what I want. I normally get up around eight in the morning and make coffee, and for about one and a half hours I sit at the desk picking the night out of my head, and searching it for inspiration. By nine thirty I have usually failed to find anything and go and feed the pigs. This takes between eight and twelve minutes. When sows have to be weaned or piglets brought into the shed for sale, it can take twice as long. This last year the rest of the morning was spent on studying the history of Cork, afternoons on farming. By half

18

four it is time for feeding the pigs again. Then, depending on the mood, I might go rambling to catch up on the gossip, and to see if there is anybody else that hates farming, which by this hour of the day I usually do. I always get depressed in the afternoon. Not the pigs' fault, though.

I hope that my business soon will be so well organised that I will be able to sit down with a clearer mind to concentrate on my poetry. As of now there is too much movement around here. I have got too many pigs: five sows and a boar, and between forty and sixty little ones. It's too intensive. Of course, not compared to, say, Denmark, where there would be seven thousand pigs on fourteen acres. Or is it seven million?

The ideal will never be reached, but two sows on fourteen acres is close to it. What I would like to do, besides writing poetry and resting my head on Damaris's lap, is to go on being a pupil of Professors Maeve and Victoria, and hopefully learn from them. In everything there is truth. I have come as close to truth with pigs as from studying the *Bhagavad-Gita*. I read in a book in the library the other day that an Irish legend says, if you drink a sow's milk you can see the wind. Wouldn't that be nice? I'll have to try it. Somebody told me that the fairies drink it out of thimbles.

Nell McDonagh

THERE WAS A time, not too long ago, when relations between the settled people and the travellers were much better than they are today. There was a need for us travellers then. Say I came to your house and mended tin cans you needed for your milking, then you were of course glad to see me. And as I had been travelling I brought with me news and stories from around the country. I had something very positive to offer. And you gave me money and food for what I did. Even up to a few decades ago there was a fairly good acceptance of travellers from the majority of the people. Today we are not very much needed anymore, and therefore people don't like to see us or know about us.

The change came very fast. One day we were basically a rural, traditional people moving around the country doing different jobs for the settled community. Then all of a sudden it was all gone. In a very short time our whole world was turned upside down. Aluminium and plastic came and replaced tin and consequently the tinsmiths, and many of the jobs we used to do as farm labourers were now done by machines. Many travellers had to move into towns and cities to look for work. At the same time many of our traditional halting-sites have been closed up, so even if we have a job to do, we have nowhere to camp. There are all those by-laws against camping. Today we travellers have a serious accommodation problem.

Not long ago, make it ten years, Navan would have been

known as a great area for spud picking. There was a lot of that type of work available to you around here. You had groups of traveller families coming from Dublin, and Leitrim, or wherever they came from. They would move into Navan and stay in Navan and pick spuds for the whole season, and then go off again. I have often seen entire families get up early in the morning to work the whole day in the potato field. It was hard work, but it was something to look forward to. I think people in general need to do something productive to feel good about themselves, and we travellers are no different. Travellers in general have a very strong work ethic. We are a proud people and we like to work and to earn our money. Today almost every little bit of economic base that we had is gone. This extremely fast change that we have seen has really destroyed a lot of our people. It didn't only take away an income, it also took away a value from us. If you are no longer required, your whole self-value will be demeaned and your pride will be gone.

Instead of doing our jobs, we got to be dependent on the dole. It was a system that was more or less forced on us; it was nothing we asked for or wished. And because we couldn't get the dole unless we had an address, we were also more or less forced to settle in one place, which was completely strange and alien to our culture.

In 1963 there was a Commission on Itinerancy. I think it was the first commission ever on itinerancy in this country. The very first line of the report was about absorption. Traveller people had to be 'absorbed' by the settled community. Let's blend them in; let's pay them money – which actually happened – to get rid of their caravans; let's pay them money to live in houses; let's give them curtains for their windows, carpets. Let's absorb them, so they won't be known as travellers. Maybe it was well meant, but isn't that a very senseless and insensitive way to try to deal with a whole group of people that has had its own traditions and its own distinctive culture for hundreds of years?

You are offering all these lovely material things to people, and of course if you offer it to a traveller woman cramped in a caravan together with six, seven, ten children, without running water, with no sanitation, with no electricity, she'll say yes, yes, we'll take a three-bedroom house with all the facilities. The only thing is that these materialistic offerings don't stop the person from being a traveller and having a traveller's particular needs.

As it is now, Ben, in order to live next door to you, the settled, I have to be somebody that I am not. For my children to be happy, they have to behave like your children, they have to speak about the same history as your children, in the same language as your children. Basically, for us to be accepted we have to deny that we are travellers. Now, I don't want to do that. I can't be something or somebody that I am not. I have seen what happens where travellers decide, 'Well, I am not allowed to be a traveller, so I'll become a settled person, and I will live like settled people live.' The price is very high. All the heritage that was given to me, I will have to lose in order to be accepted. When a person is forced to deny herself, her heritage, her identity, you get a totally unhappy person.

Ben, if you are told for long enough that you are nothing but dirt on the side of the road, unless you are a very strong person you will start believing it. You will be ashamed of being a traveller. I was ashamed, too, and I have also many times apologised meekly for actually being a traveller, but I am not doing that any more. I'm proud of being a traveller, and I want to live beside you, and I want to share society with you, but in order to do that you will have to accept me for what I am. Because you are a member of the majority of the people, you have no right to walk on me and tell me what kind of a little box I should fit into. No right whatsoever.

Ireland is a very closed society. The Irish are not used to people from different cultures. Irish culture is so homogeneous that it is easy to believe that there is only one group of people in it. People need to be educated and taught about the different communities that exist in this country. The travellers' particular history and culture should, of course, be taught and discussed in the schools. We in Ireland should learn to celebrate the differences and the diversities of cultures instead of being scared of them. If we are not prepared to do that, well, then I fear that we will not be able to live beside each other in peace. I think we have to be very much prepared to listen to each other, and each other's needs, to turn our situation into something positive and fruitful for us all.

I tell you, I like the term 'settled traveller' as little as I like 'tinkers' or 'knackers'. It is insulting to me to be called a 'settled traveller'. 'Settled traveller' is something that has been introduced into the vocabulary lately, but certainly not by us travellers, because there is no such thing as a 'settled traveller'. Many travellers live in houses today, yes, but they still have nomadic leanings and would love to take to the road if they only could. I don't know how to describe or explain it. To travel is a natural thing for us. I don't know what it is. It is something in your blood that is calling. I suppose it must be something that other nomadic people around the world are experiencing. It is something in you that urges you to move, and if you can't move you feel locked in. My father, who had spent his whole life out in the open, able to move around, decided to live in a house because he wanted to educate us and get us away from all the harshness that was put on our nomadic lifestyle by society. He got physically sick from staying in the house. He could never really adjust to being so closed in.

At one time, maybe twenty years ago, for a traveller to stay in a house or in one place all year round was something totally unheard of. Accommodation was seen more as a temporary stopping place than something permanent. Every year, come St Patrick's Day, the seventeenth of March, and whether the weather was good or bad, all the families got up and went away to do their different jobs and to meet up with extended family members at the different fairs around the country. To travel is part of our culture and lifestyle, and many of our still existing or new-found trades require mobility.

People often have this idea that the travellers historically are descendants from people who for some or other reason were dispossessed during Cromwellian times or during the Famine. It is true that some travellers originate from these periods, but not all of us. The travellers' history is much older than that. We have our own language. The official name is Shelta, but we call it Cant, or some call it Gammon. One theory is that this secret language was picked up by itinerant bards and metalworkers in the early centuries when they went into the monasteries to do jobs for the cloistered monks, to repair cutlery or crockery or whatever they did. Somehow we seem to be descendants from these itinerant bards or tradespeople. There are also references to 'tinkers' in Irish documents from the twelfth century. That will give you an idea about how far back we go. The closest similarity we have to Cant is Old Irish, the language that was spoken in Ireland before the twelfth century. Somebody might think that we are gypsies, but that is not so. The gypsies and the travellers have different cultures and different histories. We are different people, even though the English gypsies brought us the canvas-covered 'barrel-top' wagon when they briefly came to Ireland during the First World War to escape conscription.

There are roughly 24,000 travellers in Ireland. Again people say 'travellers' and they think every traveller is the same, but these 24,000 people are divided into three different main groupings. There is a small grouping which is the 'fair-people' – you know, show-business people, who do the fairs and the carnivals. Another grouping is made of people who became travellers at the time of the Famine. Before that they were settled people themselves. They have the closest links with the settled community of all the travellers. The biggest group, which I belong to, is more traditional. When I say traditional, I mean our customs and our culture.

Some of our customs are very particular. I know it is a bit strange to note that at the end of the twentieth century we have a group of people who arrange marriages within a very limited sphere, but that is what we 'traditional' travellers do. All our marriages are arranged, arranged not only within the main group of 'traditional' travellers, but even arranged in our own family-grouping. For example, my family-grouping would be made up of McDonaghs, Joyces, Collinses, Reillys. I suppose we would be a couple of thousand people altogether. We who belong to this family-grouping would only move within its circle. You would not get some of our family going down to, say, Wexford to intermarry with the Connors or the Cashes, because that is their family-grouping. You stay within your own group, and there is where you do all your dealings. The 'fair-people' and the travellers descending from the Famine all choose their own partners, and they wouldn't live in big extended families like we 'traditionals' do.

However, there are some changes occurring in the traveller community. In recent years there have been intermarriages between the 'traditionals' and the 'fair-people'. Until recently that was something unheard of. And in our family we have relatives who are married to the settled community. A couple of years ago when it happened, it was a great shock, and people were saying that that was the worst thing that could ever happen, but now it is accepted.

So, some things are changing, but others seem to be pretty watertight. For example, the moral code amongst travellers is very very strongly rooted. Especially the code concerning sex is of very great importance. From the age of twelve, the girls within our community are chaperoned everywhere. You wouldn't get a girl of twelve or thirteen being allowed to walk down to town by herself. If anything happened with her, say that she slipped down the ditch with somebody, it would be more than a scandal. It wouldn't affect only the two people involved, it would affect the whole family-grouping. Nobody would inter-marry with them, nobody would want to know them. There is no grey area there. It's all black and white. I suppose it is a method of protection for the group and the family. It holds us together. Okay, maybe at times it can be very strict, and it can be very severe too, but when you grow up knowing and being aware of something of this character, it is not such a great shock or restriction on your life. It is there as a part of your life from the time you grow up.

Because we follow these old traditions and customs doesn't mean we are some kind of freaks. I mean, matched marriages were very common in rural Ireland at least up until this century. We are not that different from other Irish people. We are not a different race; we only have a different culture. My husband served in the UN peace-keeping force in Lebanon, and my great-grandfather fought in the Boer War. That sounds pretty normal and reassuring, doesn't it? And I tell you, when Ireland plays soccer we cheer the team and we are proud when it wins and sad when it loses, just like anybody else in this country. We are travellers and we are Irish.

You have a lot of travellers abroad too, about 15,000 in Britain, and at least 10,000 in the United States, mainly in the southern states. The travellers who went to America did it during the Famine, but they would have been travellers already before they left. They didn't become travellers because of the Famine. They speak Cant, marry within their own group and in general they live a traditional traveller's life.

It will be interesting to see what happens to our children in the future. They talk more and more about going to universities and getting different jobs. That is good, of course, but sometimes I fear for them that they will get more and more settled, and that they won't feel any more what it is to be a traveller. I want my children to know their history and to be proud of it and of their culture, and I hope they will find reason to continue to be a part of it and not just feel confused about who they are. I have great hope, though, for the travellers' future. The traveller population is very young, and it is growing, and many are now going to schools. I think that the generation that grows up now will be very educated and politicised. Soon the settled community won't be able to kick us around any more.

There are a lot of negative feelings created around travellers today. There are still many settled people that are very good with the travellers and accept them, but the majority of people don't want travellers at all any more. You mention the word 'traveller' in Ireland today and you will create the most sophisticated residents' associations in the world. You can have a residents' association lying dormant for years, there can be a severe drug-problem in the area, there can be a lack of housing in the area, there can be a big problem with unemployment, but not a whisper will be heard. Nobody will get up protesting about it. But mention that travellers are going to move into an area and suddenly all the residents' associations are waking up, and in no time they are out there marching and shouting and lobbying their politicians or council officials.

There is a proposed halting-site in Navan. You know, a properly serviced halting-site, equipped with sanitation, running water, electricity, refuse collection, and so on. As a result of this proposal, we now have a twenty-four hour vigil on the site. People have come out of their homes to sit up whole nights in rain, sleet, hail or snow, to stop any work that the council has tried to begin, because they don't want travellers. These people can't have any pride at all.

Do you know that the infant mortality rate of the traveller babies is three times greater than that of the settled community? Do you know that the life expectancy of a traveller woman is twelve years less than of a settled woman, and eleven years less for a traveller man? And that is today, and not a statistic from a hundred years ago. It is a very frightening statistic, but not very surprising. Travellers are treated like vermin in Ireland today. They don't spray us with pesticides, that is true, but they spray us with slurry. Just read the papers any day and you will know a little bit of the violence that is going on against the travellers. And society as a whole doesn't seem to care too much about it. It's a shame.

There are about 1,200 traveller families living beside the roads, in conditions that remind you of the refugee camps that you see on television from African countries. No cosy Ireland here, miste'. More than half of the 600 traveller families living in the greater Dublin area, which means several thousand people, live without their own toilet, and two-thirds without electricity!

Ben, I have known politicians that have lost their seats in the councils because they stood up in defence of travellers. It is not a very popular issue as you can imagine. There are very few men and women out there who are prepared to stand up for us.

When the first group of houses for travellers was built here in Navan, the residents actually brought the case to the High Court to object to it. The usual prejudiced talk you hear is, that if travellers move into an area the property will be devalued because nobody wants to live beside travellers. If that is true, it shows how sick the situation is. The talk also goes that the crime rate in the area will increase. That is totally untrue. The figures are there; you can check them with the Gardaí if you want. You also hear that the travellers are drinking a lot, but again check the figures and you'll find that the incidence of alcoholism is in fact lower among the traveller community than among the general population. You will also usually hear that women and girls are in danger because of these traveller men, which again is totally untrue. Yes, there are many rapes in this country, but very few are committed by traveller men.

Ben, I have heard these prejudices so many times that I am full of it! It has all to do with ignorance and fear. Ignorance breeds fear and prejudice. I don't say that the fear isn't real, only that it is unjustified. It is a vicious circle which is very difficult to break, but we have to. I have asked hundreds of people who have marched against us if they know any traveller and if they have ever spoken to a traveller, and they all say no. Maybe we should start there, to meet and to talk to each other?

Pat Buckley

I WANTED TO BE a priest from the time I was very young, but my desire to be a priest was very romantic and I didn't realise what the Church was really like until I became a part of the clergy. There is still a lot about the Church and the religion that is precious to me. I like the liturgy, I like mass and the celebrations, the rituals, the music, the smells, the incense, the robes and the candles. It is a spiritual thing. The mass and the liturgy and the rituals speak to something within me. I think that every person needs some kind of ritual. Even in England, where it is now a pagan country if you like, they have the ritual of the queen marching up and down.

I think human beings need ritual as a part of their spiritual nourishment. I also obviously like the Bible and the scriptures. I don't interpret them literally, but I think that the scriptures are inspiring. I like the long history of spirituality that exists in the Christian Church, I like the mystical people and the mystical writers. I also like some of the good things that the Church has done for people in more practical ways, like providing medical care and food for the hungry. I always like to stress the fact that I am not an enemy of the Church, which so many people seem to think, and that I am very proud of being a Catholic priest.

But I also see the Church as an organisation which can always be improved. Just like every day I have to try to improve myself, I can also try and improve my family, which is the Church. And it needs to improve, a lot. Over the years I have discovered that

31

the Church is also a human organisation, and that it is very much about power and money. I don't like the power structure that has developed inside the Church. It can be very wicked and very ruthless. My own case is a proof of that.

I worked in Divis Flats in West Belfast for five years. I worked very much with young people there. I organised youth clubs, and so on. I was also trying to get better housing for the area. Divis Flats was very dirty. It was a very run down place in a very republican area, a place to where the police never came. It had graffiti painted all over the walls, there was rubbish everywhere – burnt-out cars, mattresses, rats, dead rats, shitty nappies – everything just lying everywhere. I kept thinking to myself for a year, 'What can I do to begin to raise the spirits of these people?' Something had to be done because life was miserable there. One night I had a brainwave. It was the simplest thing, a thing that I hoped would have a knock-on effect: we should start with cleaning up the streets and the buildings! I got a lot of shovels and brushes and paint and overalls from the government, and one morning at nine o'clock I put on my overalls and went out on the street outside the church with a brush and a shovel and started sweeping. Very soon windows opened and people were looking out to see what the priest, God's servant, was doing. Then people started to come out and help me with it. At the end of the week there were 500 people sweeping, cleaning and painting. The whole place was transformed. After two weeks the man from the gas company came to fix a pipe and thought he was in the wrong place. When all was finished we had a big festival for three days. The whole thing certainly raised the spirits and morale in the area, although not for everybody.

The priests that I was living in the house with were very cross with me. On one of the first days of this project, they said to me when I went in for dinner: 'You weren't ordained to become a fucking binman. You are letting the priesthood down.' They thought I was crazy, and when I went back out after dinner that day to continue with the cleaning, they came to the window and they were giving me the two-finger sign and were making faces at me. The next thing that happened was that they refused to tolerate me in the dining-room, so I had to eat in the kitchen with the housekeepers and the cleaners. That was fine for me; I didn't mind. I was hurt by what my colleagues did to me, of course, but I was happier in the kitchen with the staff, because they were nice people.

What also had happened during this time, and this also made my colleagues cross, was that when I came to the parish I told the people of Divis Flats on my first Sunday there that I was their friend, and that they could come to me any time they needed me, day or night. The other priests didn't like this, because they themselves had certain hours to see people. People coming ringing the bell at any time of the day or night was disturbing them. They liked to drink their coffee and brandy in peace. Then I suggested I could put my own bell on the door, but they wouldn't allow that either, because that would have given me special rights.

I used to have tea at six o'clock every night and at half six there was always a lot of people waiting to see me – and nobody waited to see the other priests. They were jealous about this. They called it my 'surgery'. They disliked me more and more, and finally I was beaten up physically. It sounds completely crazy, and it was. It happened like this. One night there was a girl from the area in seeing me. Her dad had just died and she hadn't slept for a week. She was there to talk to me about her

33

grief. During the conversation she fainted. I went to the priests' dining-room next door to get her a glass of water. As I went in, the parish priest came down the stairs and he saw the girl lying across the desk where I had put her, and he must have presumed I had done something to her, sexually, I think, because he had a big hang-up about women, so he said to me from half-way up the stairs: 'Would you mind telling me what is going on in this fucking house?' 'I will, if you ask me properly,' I told him. So he ran down the stairs and grabbed me by the lapels and shoved me back through the dining-room and onto the floor, where he started punching and kicking me. He screamed to me that he was going to report me to the bishop. I said to him that I hoped he would report this assault too. The next morning he was crying and said that he was sorry, so I let it all pass. A couple of years later, when I had a conversation with the then bishop, now Cardinal Daly, about this, he told me he didn't believe that it had happened, and that I was mentally ill and that I had made this up.

I suppose from quite early in my career I would not co-operate or be obedient to what I saw as a ruthless system, and obviously that made many react to me. I kept saying what I believed in and doing what I believed a good Christian should do. Eventually it led to various reports about me, and one day I was called to Bishop Daly. He had taken a very negative view of me. He felt I was too involved in social issues, and that I was also talking to journalists too much. 'In the future when I look out over the ocean of priests, I don't want to see your head above the waves,' he said. When I didn't follow his order but kept popping my head up, he started to move me around from parish to parish. This is often how the hierarchy acts when it wants to silence somebody.

It came to a point when Bishop Daly offered me £5,000 to move to America. He thought I would fit in better over there. When I wouldn't go, he flatly sacked me from the church I was serving in, but I refused to leave the house in which I was living, and which was owned by the Catholic Church. By now my dispute with the Church had become very public, because I had understood that if I fought it in private they would wipe me out, and I would have had to move from here. They would have given me no money, and I would have had to go home and live with my parents or something like that. Basically I would have vegetated. They would have loved that to happen. The hierarchy relishes any opponent's or critic's disintegration.

I didn't let them intimidate me. Instead of backing off, I brought Bishop Daly to court for sacking me. I won the case, though for different legal intricacies it never really became a case, but I won in the sense that I succeeded in getting a bishop to court. And I am now, nine or ten years later, still in the same house. I think it has come as a great surprise to Cardinal Daly that after so long I am still here. He thought he had seen the last of me when he sacked me. At the time I was very cheeky and told him that I would still be here when he was gone. The hierarchy would love to kick me out of this house too, but they know I would chain myself to the radiators or do something drastic like that, and in no time at all the media would be on the spot. I think they are shrewd enough to avoid that. One thing the Catholic Church doesn't want today is bad publicity. They have more than enough of that already.

During many of these years, I was pretty alone. Many of my colleagues avoided me and crossed over to the other side of the street when they saw me, but I also got some supportive letters from priests from around the island. Many of them agreed with me in my criticism of the Church and joined me in many of my opinions, but most of them were afraid to say it out loud. I hadn't expected much else. In general, in Ireland, the ordinary priest is very subservient to the hierarchy. Not strange, as the priest school is more like a priest factory. The nearest example I have ever seen to the priest factory was when I was working in Kilkeel in County Down. My parishioners had a fish factory. The herrings came in at one end of the factory, they had their head chopped off, they had their guts removed and they had their backbone taken out, and then you had your fillets of herrings. And this is what is happening at the priest factory. The guys come in, they take away their brains so they can't think, they take away their guts so they can't stand up. The hierarchy only wants silent sheep in its flock. If some black sheep enter the flock, they can't cope with it and they do anything to get rid of them.

Today I run my own independent ministry in the house. I took out a wall and made an oratory of two rooms with seats for seventy people. I have a lot of freedom now. I can still be a priest and I can still do things to help people. And whatever I do I don't need to worry about who is watching me. To get a 'normal' job now as a priest would be like going back to prison.

Most days I celebrate mass for a small number of people who come here. I also do a lot of work with divorced people. I remarry divorced people. Their problem is that the Church won't remarry them, because the Church doesn't accept a second marriage. I, being a priest, can still solemnise marriage. I remain a priest and nobody and nothing, not even the pope, however Godlike he thinks he is, can stop me from being a priest. Once ordained a priest, forever a priest. I could solemnise a marriage even if I became a disgraced priest. Once you are ordained and once you celebrate a marriage according to the rites of the Catholic Church, then that marriage is valid in canon law as well as in civil law. The people that I marry do not only want to get married legally according to civil law, which they could do in a registry office, but they also want the spiritual side of the marriage ceremony. I satisfy both the legal and the religious ceremony. I marry about 200 couples a year. Most of them are couples from the Republic, but there are also couples from here in Northern Ireland, or from England, and sometimes from the Continent or from other parts of the world. This activity is, of course, not at all liked by the Catholic Church.

I was twenty-six years of age when I came to Divis Flats. I was full of idealism. I gave of myself 103 per cent and burned my candles at both ends. A few years ago I got Crohn's disease and had to have three parts of my bowels removed. I was probably pushing myself too hard. What I have done now is that I have curtailed my expenditure of energy slightly. I have tried to make a little bit more space for myself so I won't burn out completely, but I am still very idealistic and I am still very much for people, and if people need me I want to be available. I would expend any amount of effort and energy on helping any one person. Just before you came today, I had a lady belonging to the Church of Ireland coming to talk to me about getting married soon to a Catholic. She asked what they were going to do about their marriage, about their children, and so on. Earlier this morning another lady rang me. She was in an awful state. She was changing her little son's nappy when she discovered that he had got an erection. She was wondering had she done anything wrong or had she given birth to a future pervert. So, you see, people do contact me for big things, and for little things. I suppose I am, as I think a priest should be, available, accessible. If people have a problem I want them to feel that they can come to me and know that they won't be condemned or lectured by me, but instead that I will listen to them and try to help them. And people do come to me from all over Ireland. I do a lot of counselling.

Many people have said to me that my main problem has been that I was ahead of my time. Now time seems to be catching up, but I would still be a little bit ahead of it in my thinking, and maybe especially in my actions. I know that there are many priests with good progressive ideas out there, but still today very few of them dare to put them into practice. They are still too scared to challenge the hierarchy.

Recently I have started to give blessings to gay couples. I had to think my way through to doing that, but if a couple wants to come to me to have God's blessing and to have their rings blessed and to ask God to help them to be good people, then they are welcome. I can see no reason why I should shut the door to them.

I also think that priests should be allowed to marry if they wish. I think that contraception is a matter for couples between themselves, and not for the Church to decide on. I don't like abortion much, but I think there are circumstances in which it is very understandable. I also think that the Church needs to be more compassionate to its members who are homosexuals. There are a host of issues like that, moral issues, about which I would have a very liberal and tolerant approach. The approach of the Church would be much more dogmatic. In fact, the Church is far too dogmatic to have any importance in the ruling of a complex society. To run a modern society on the Church's rules would be like trying to run a spaceship on turf.

The role of the Church in Ireland has been changing dramatically in the last ten years. It has been losing a lot of its power –

not all, but a lot of it. I think that is good. The Church and the priest has been put on pedestals for far too long, and now they are falling. I think all these sex scandals that are revealed every day, with priests and bishops involved, are graces from God. It is high time that these scandals, that have been happening for years and hundred of years, come out into the open.

Up until recently the priests and the bishops were pretending that they were perfect and that they were gods, but many of us, both inside and outside the Church system, knew that that wasn't the case, and now they have been caught literally with their trousers down. Now they are seen as being as interested in sex as every other human being, and they are as weak as everybody else. This has taken away a lot of the priests' and bishops' pride and arrogance. Hopefully that will stop them lecturing to married couples about sexuality, because people will say: 'Physician, heal thyself!'

For people to understand the seriousness and the depth of this gigantic change, they have to understand the role the Church has had, and in many ways still has, in Ireland. The priests have been the masters here. The priest was seen as the Almighty God. Ireland has been called a priest-ridden country, and it has been priest-ridden, because the priest was the boss of everything. He was in charge of the parish, in charge of the village, in charge of the school, in charge of the hospital, chairman of the football club, and so on and so on. Everything that happened had the priest as boss or chairman. Ireland was so absolutely Catholic that even the dogs stopped eating meat during Lent. If you had a problem, you went to the priest with it. Even if it was about a broken leg, the doctor was second to the priest. The Church had enormous power. Therefore, all these scandals which are now revealed in the media about priests that have come into your home with the sole intention of seducing and abusing your children, are a terrible blow to the authority of the Church.

I am sure you have heard about Brendan Smyth, this priest that has sexually abused so many children. He is one of the people in Ireland now that everybody loves to hate. I can understand that, but to me it is very irrational. It is true that he has done things that are very wrong and inexcusable, and it is right that he should be in prison and that his victims are the ones who deserve the most thought and compassion, but having said that, there is also a sense in which he himself is the victim. He needs punishment, but he also needs help. It is said that 80 per cent of the people who sexually abuse children were sexually abused themselves when they were young. I don't know if that is a true figure or if it is the case for Brendan Smyth, but I know that he is a victim of a system that for years and years has forced people into a very unhealthy repression of their sexuality.

The Catholic Church has always had a very negative view on sex, and it trained all its people, but particularly all its priests, in the same very negative way. In our training all of us were very distorted and twisted in our attitude to sex, and we were given huge hang-ups and feelings of guilt.

I am forty-three years of age. I never had any sex instruction in my life. Sex was always a big mystery to me. When I got to puberty, I started thinking about sex and I obviously started experimenting with myself, but then I was told immediately, in confessions and in sermons, that that was a mortal sin. I remember one priest telling me in confession that every time I did something with myself, I killed 200,000 people. It was like a holocaust in the mind every time I touched myself. Imagine the guilt. It was huge. It was very negative, and it unfortunately was very common. It was not only me it happened to. You can imagine the type of frustration and unhappiness and twistedness that follows when you impose that regime on people and on a society. When you do that you are really looking for trouble.

We were never taught about sex in our training to become priests, as we weren't taught how to be celibate. The subject was basically ignored. It was an embarrassment. We were told about sin, and that everything sexual was sin. We had to keep going to confession if we had 'bad thoughts', or 'bad actions' with ourselves. Every morning for ten minutes before daily mass, the spiritual director of the seminary sat in a little room at the back of the chapel to hear the confessions of those who had 'sinned' during the night. 'When temptation strikes, grasp the crucifix,' he said.

I was conscious in the seminary that people occasionally had sex with each other, and I would have known students that on their rare days off seemed to have girlfriends, but at that age you are very idealistic and you want to be a priest and you think that the bishops and the superiors are right, and you think that the problems are with yourself, that you are weak and evil. It is very difficult to cope with it. To take hundreds and thousands of people and make them priests or nuns or brothers, and tell them that they are never allowed to enjoy the gift of sex, neither with another person nor with themselves, or that they can never have a sexual thought, is so bad. I think that when people are forced to suppress their sexuality, it throws up all kind of aberrations. We see it today when the lid is taken off. We have a very sick situation. A priest said to me recently: 'We weren't allowed to get rid of our semen, so it went to our brain and made us mad.' It looks like he could be right.

I am just reading *Sex, Priests and Power* by the American priest, Richard Sipe. He says that at least 6 per cent of Catholic

41

priests abuse children. That would make a few hundred pae-dophile priests in Ireland alone. Sipe's comment about why the American bishops haven't tackled the problem there is that they are themselves abusers. I have personally seen and heard too much to let that surprise me.

Sipe proves further that around 60 per cent of priests are involved sexually with adults, around 20 per cent of them with men and about 40 per cent with women. I am not surprised by this high number, either. After it was revealed that Bishop Casey, the former bishop of Galway – who is now stationed by the Church somewhere in the jungle of Guatemala – had a son in a secret relationship, I started this little group we call 'Bethany'. It is a group for women that have had, or have, rela-tionships with priests. It is a loose support group. If a woman rings me, let's say from Dublin, and tells me her story, then I will put her in contact with three or four other women that find themselves in the same situation, so they can begin to meet for friendship and support. There are almost a hundred women in the group now, and it is constantly growing. Some of them have had relationships with a priest for twenty years. Some of them have children together with a priest. Sometimes abortion has been a part of the relationship, paid for by the priest. The hier-archy still pretends that these cases are only once-off cases. Anybody that says differently is only 'trying to spread malicious rumours and to blacken the Church'.

The Church has always, and until recently very successfully, tried to cover up all these types of affairs. The whole thing has been about keeping power, keeping secrecy and keeping the so-called good name of the Church, and it didn't matter a damn about the victims.

Jim McAllister

I WAS BORN ON the square here just three doors away. My parents had seven children. I am the only child left in Ireland. The rest of them are in America and Britain. I was in Britain too for a long time.

I am not even sure how long my family has been in this town, but certainly for quite a few generations. I know that in some records of the town there were several McAllister families, and some of them had obvious Scots-type first names. For example, there was an Archibald. Turley could also be Scottish, but more likely to be in the Gaelic-Scots tradition than in the British-Scots tradition. My father was a great local historian, but he died suddenly when I was young and I never got around to discussing all these things with him. I know for a fact that our branch of the family originally lived in Roche, beside Roche Castle in County Louth across the border. How it came that we moved I don't know. We had land there and were dispossessed in one shape or fashion.

I am not sure if we arrived here immediately after that, or what happened to my family's religious affiliations. I have Protestant relations in this area. The caretaker of the old cemetery up the road, a cousin of mine, is Protestant, and I have both Catholic and Protestant relatives buried there. I know that many families 'took the soup' during the Famine. The choice for many was that either you remained a Catholic and died of starvation, or you 'took the soup' and became a Protestant, and lived.

43

Maybe that is what happened to some of my family. It doesn't really matter. Religion has no bearing on the matter up here at all. The Protestants in the area live the same life as the rest of us. They drink in the same pubs, etc, and they mourn the same victims of the conflict. It is only used by some people or some groups for their own purposes. It is a part of the divide-and-conquer tactic. The British Empire has done the same elsewhere, in Africa, in India. They divided people by colour, or by caste, and set one against the other. Here they have done it on the grounds of religion.

The reality is often that many Protestants in the North don't like to address where their Protestantism comes from. They see Protestantism equated with Britishness. Actually it isn't. Many who now think that they are British would have roots the same as mine, or even, my roots might be more British than theirs, if you go back far enough. The president of the GAA, the Gaelic Athletic Association, the main sporting body in Ireland, which is a nationalist body, is a Protestant from County Wicklow. He is quite happy to be an Irishman. He doesn't think he is British.

There has always been hardship here, because areas like this were studiously avoided by the government or the governmental agencies when it came to development or anything like that. Of course, many parts of Ireland or of the Republic would be the same. Emigration has been our main occupation for generations, and it is not that much different today.

This is an area that never had industry, that never had anything. People here have always had to, in many ways, survive on their wits, and they are very good at it. If you look around the area you see nice houses and cars and whatever else, and you know it is not a completely impoverished area, even though there is very little regular work around. Because the state never really looked after people in this type of area, people have learnt to look after themselves and to look after their friends and neighbours. We live on a border. Smuggling has been a natural occupation for a significant number of people here. The people around here wouldn't in any shape or form despise a smuggler or look down upon him or see him as doing anything wrong. It would be a bit like: 'Would you let your daughter marry a smuggler?' 'Is he a good smuggler?'

Historically you had men sent from this area to deal with oppressors in other parts of Ireland. They were hired to execute landlords and their agents, not only in South Armagh, but also in County Monaghan and County Louth and as far as County Meath.

Most people would only call this a village, although it's designated a small market town. The border runs right through the parish. Crossmaglen is known as the parish of Uppercracken. There are three churches in Uppercracken: Crossmaglen, Glasdrummond and Shelagh. Shelagh is in County Louth across the border. So, according to the law, this parish is in two countries. It is in the Republic of Ireland and in the United Kingdom.

My wife came from Shelagh. She came from about a mile and a half from where I was born. We were neighbours. We grew up together. Her school and my school had sports competitions and things like that, but the law says she and I were foreigners to each other. This is how ludicrous the situation is.

If you go around the town of Crossmaglen, or Forkill, or any of the villages in this area, and you get a survey of the households, I think that you probably find that in the marriages or partnerships sixty, maybe seventy per cent would have one of the partners coming from across the border, from either County Monaghan or County Louth. There would even be a few from

45

further afield: Kerry, Meath, Kildare. Very very few come from say Newry or Armagh city or elsewhere northward, because the natural life of this area has always been directed west or south. When we were young fellows, and I would say it is the same today, and going out socialising, we either went to Dundalk in County Louth, or to Carrickmacross or Castleblaney in County Monaghan. We wouldn't go to Warrenpoint, for example. I only remember going to Newry, which is only eighteen miles from here, to a dance once in my whole life. And that has nothing to do with politics; that's how the land is, and how the tradition and everything else is. Even the British governing this area for several centuries as an entity would go south to Monaghan for their outings.

Much of the social life today is cut across in many ways because of the border and the political situation. It doesn't stop the social life, but it poses some difficulties. The same for a farmer. The land of many farmers from around here crosses the border. It means they have two sets of bureaucracies to deal with, two sets of documents.

We have burial grounds in this area that date back 5,000 years, and we have lots of old forts. There is a history of habitation here going back thousands and thousands of years, and many of the myths and sagas and legends of Ireland have a focus in this area. Like Cúchulainn, for instance, probably our most heroic warrior ever. He got his name from the mountain in the background here – Slieve Gullion. Nobody goes around thinking about these things, naturally enough, but I think it is there, in the psyche. We know who we are, we know we belong here, we know we will always be here no matter what happens, whereas the British soldiers won't be.

Not only that. People in this area know each other, warts and all. One of the things about rural life, and you probably discovered this when you came to live in Ireland, is that people know everything about everybody. There is no point in trying to pretend that you are somebody that you aren't. They know who your granny was, your great-grandfather, and so on. It can be annoying sometimes, but in the situation that we up here are living in it is helpful. For example, take the supergrass phenomenon, where the British army and the RUC recruited informers in Belfast and Derry from within the IRA. We never got one in South Armagh. Again because everybody knows everybody. The IRA can pick and choose here. I would say, for every twenty people who apply to join the IRA here, they probably take only one. They know who they want and they choose him.

You are talking about roughly 1,600 people living here in the town. Up in the barracks there would be around 400 British soldiers. We didn't see any change at all in British military activity during the ceasefire. There were as many British soldiers as ever. This is probably the heaviest fortified area in the whole of Ireland. I mean rural Ireland: West Belfast and parts of Derry would be just the same. It is an exceedingly large base for such a small town. It is certainly about 150 metres long, and 150 metres deep. It is a large military fortification, a modern version of the old forts you would see in the Wild West. In fact, the British call the one up here Fort Alamo. They put those type of names on their bases around Northern Ireland. I suppose they see themselves in these far-flung outposts as being amongst the savages to some degree.

Around the base you have got a very very high perimeter fence. That is just an iron fence. Behind that they have got blast walls, reinforced-steel concrete, tapered walls, five to six feet thick. These blast walls have actually worked against the British.

When the IRA discovered that the walls didn't allow bombs to go through, they realised they could instead put the bomb inside first and then let it explode and the walls would keep the blast in.

On the corners of the base you have got a number of watch-towers, specially constructed steel towers, again because they have been blown up or burnt so many times in the past. Some of them are over 100 foot high. They are looking over the whole town. Then you have got a number of nests of cameras at street level to watch the people walking around the streets, and to watch the cars coming. And higher up in the air you have got a nest of four cameras to survey the surrounding countryside. In addition to that, knowing that we are constantly overflown and checked by helicopters and listened to by different listening devices, you realise that George Orwell when he wrote *Nineteen Eighty-Four* didn't even know the half of it.

There hasn't been a lot said about it in the media, but during the Troubles there have been many visitors to Crossmaglen and other places in the North from abroad, looking at and studying how to control a people. We are talking about modern high tech. There is a big market for it around the world, and Britain is making money on it. Britain is one of the biggest exporters of the technology of repression in the world. Here they have a per-fectly real show-ground for their products. It couldn't be better for them. Of course, that plays its part in the conflict in Northern Ireland, and in its solution, and in the will to find a solution. It's like with the British soldiers. This is a perfect hos-tile environment to train them in. At home in Britain they would just lay around drinking beer. No doubt that is another motive for the British to stay.

Over the years that this latest conflict has gone on, which is over a quarter of a century now, the British have taken over much of the property in the town to extend their barracks. They have taken the back gardens of many houses. The laws that the British forces have here allow them to do basically anything they like. I think it is Section 19 of the EPA, the Emergency Provisions Act, that states that the Crown Forces – the police and the soldiers – can variously occupy, seize or destroy property, they can restrict or close down access or right of way, they can stop and detain people, they can do anything they want. And they have done. An example: Paddy McKeogh was an old farmer from around here. When he retired he moved into town and built a good little bungalow up beside where the police station or the original barracks was at the time. He was unlucky because the Troubles broke out shortly after, and immediately the British evicted him from his bungalow and made it a part of the barracks.

Up to today they have taken the back gardens of almost all the houses opposite the square, and they took a large portion of the Gaelic football pitch, the Rangers' football pitch. That is fairly well known these days. The Dublin government have spoken about it in the past. To take people's back gardens is bad, but to take the pitch is even worse. Your back garden is part of your home, I know, but to some degree the football pitch is, as in most of our Irish villages, the centre of the community. Much of the community life revolves around the football club. When you attack that and take their property, you are even doing worse than taking somebody's back garden.

There is no positive contact whatsoever between the people in the base and us out here. No nods, no winks, no good mornings. The people here wouldn't sell a box of matches or serve a cup of tea to a soldier or a policeman, and that's been the same since certainly within a few months of them arriving here. This attitude wasn't forced on people. The people took this decision themselves. I don't think it was difficult. You see, what is supposed to be our government, what is supposed to be our police force, what is supposed to be our army, we don't see them as ours at all. We see them as people who in many ways have caused the problems, and as people who have no real interest in addressing the problems. We see them as our enemies.

People have to live in this context, and people do that in many different ways. One of the basic ways is that daily life is lived as if none of this applied at all. If you tried to live your life around the base and around the outposts – there are three more big bases and nineteen smaller outposts around South Armagh, an area of a couple of hundred square miles – recognising them all the time and worrying about them all the time, you would crack up. You have got to live almost as if they weren't there. You know they are there and you try to remove them, but you act in your own personal life as if this wasn't happening. There is a man down town here, Paddy Short, who has a wonderful turn of phrase. One time somebody asked Paddy how the local people react to the soldiers, and Paddy said: 'The Brits, you wouldn't even ignore them.' To ignore them would be to recognise them.

There is a great degree of truth in that but, nonetheless, this whole situation infects your life all the time, whether you like it or not. You have the helicopters hovering over your roof, you are stopped on the road, or the soldiers are walking through your farm, or through your back garden or whatever. My mother is up there in the square. She is eighty-five. She has been heartbroken for years, because she can't keep the garden any more. I used to do the garden for her, you know, some flowers and vegetables. We just abandoned it, because every day soldiers come climbing over the wall and walking through, and you can't stop them. I have had rows with them, and fights with them. It isn't worth it, it gets you nowhere – though it might get you somewhere. It often does. I have been taken to Gough Barracks in Armagh city, where they have a major interrogation centre, several times. I have been there three or four times for three days, and I have been in the local barracks and police barracks numerous times for three to four hours. I have been threatened, I have had the house raided, everything looked at, personal letters read. They storm in with muddy boots on and just leave a mess after them. Dirt everywhere. In some houses they actually smash up things, pull up floorboards and break them or whatever. I never had that, but I know many people that had. They do it to hassle and to intimidate people. Even common sense would tell them that if I was an IRA member I wouldn't hide any weapon at home. I don't believe that they have ever found anything in a house in South Armagh. Most people in the area would have had some experience of this harassment, but when you are well known, as I am since becoming a Sinn Féin councillor, you probably get more of it. But even before I was publicly involved in politics, it happened to me. I was still lucky. Some people from around here have been badly hurt.

The IRA wouldn't have a total, but would have a very very high, support around here. You have actually got the scenario that, if you look at the Sinn Féin/SDLP vote, it is roughly fifty-fifty, but the IRA's support is different. Their support is much higher than that. The bottom line is that, if there is a choice to be made between the British army and the IRA, even people who vote for the SDLP, and who wouldn't be out and out

51

supporters of the IRA, would choose the IRA. For instance, if the British army are hiding soldiers on some farmer's land, now, that farmer may well be a nationalist or a republican, maybe an SDLP-voter, he mightn't even be political at all, but that farmer will invariably make sure that some republicans are made aware that there are soldiers dug in or hiding on his property. The reverse doesn't happen. If they see the IRA they will not tell the British army. This is not something people around here are forced to do. They wouldn't have to tell the IRA that there were soldiers there unless they made that conscious choice. The British could be on your land and you wouldn't even know they were there. In fact, when the IRA mount an operation, they will spend a long long time checking out the whole area they will have to go through. There will be hundreds of men and women out, walking through the fields and checking out everything to make sure there are no soldiers there.

This support depends, I think, on a combination of things. One thing is that even if some people from here wouldn't be supporters of the IRA they would see them as local. It is also in the nature of the area, and in the history of the area, as I mentioned before, but the number one thing is: this is an Irish area, no question about that. You see no tokens of Britishness or loyalism anywhere in this area. Everything you see here reminds you that you are in Ireland.

The origin of the recent conflict is the same origin of the conflict that always was in Ireland with the British. The fact that you used the word 'recent' in your question is very important, because it is recent. It is not the first conflict. It is the same conflict we have had for centuries. In particular since 1798 when Wolfe Tone gave us the idea of republicanism from the French Revolution. Before that there were many conflicts but they were basically nationalist conflicts. It had more to do with who will be your king or who will be your ruler. Republicanism has more to do with the kind of society you want, what type of structures, etc. One of the main differences is that nationalism sees the vision of a united Ireland as something that would be nice. A bit like winning the lotto or something like that. It wouldn't be the immediate goal. Republicanism believes that you can work and live far better with a united Ireland. We believe that Ireland north, south, east and west can never develop properly until we have a united economy and united political structures and a governmental structure. Even in the modern context with the EU and the limiting of the government's power, we still believe that a united Ireland is in fact the only way forward for Ireland, and something that should be achieved as quickly as possible.

The unionists say that they don't want to join the Republic of Ireland, or the Free State as they call it. I don't want to join it either. I want to be part of a new Republic. I think a new context would be good for the whole of Ireland, and when it happens one and a half million new people will come into the country, in many ways a very radical and political people.

Billy Hutchinson

I WAS BORN HERE in Shankill in Belfast and I have lived here my whole life. My family was planted here from Scotland during the time of Elizabeth I in the beginning of the colonial era. My father's side of the family came from Edinburgh and my mother's side came from around the Scottish Highlands. So my family has been here in the north-east part of Ireland from around 1603. I have a long history in this country and to say to me, as I sometimes hear people saying, to go back from where I came, I think that is both stupid and wrong. I am home. Northern Ireland is part of the United Kingdom and that's where I was born and where I have lived all my life.

I'm British. What makes me feel British is of course that I was born of British parents in the British state and when I went to school I was taught British history and British customs. I have been brought up in a community which, for example, was very proud of its military service with the British forces, and in a tradition that respected the people who were not conscripted but volunteered to go out fighting in the two world wars and other conflicts around the world, like Aden, Cyprus, Belize, the Falklands. I was also brought up supporting an English football team. I support Leeds United and I have done that since I was a little child. I visit England quite regularly and I have an affinity with people there, especially with the working-class people or people from the same socio-economic background as me, in Manchester, Leeds, London. I have a bond with English people and I communicate with them all the time. I also get my Britishness from the television I watch. The BBC brings the news into my home, what is happening in Northern Ireland and Great Britain, and also shows me the culture of the rest of the people who live in the United Kingdom. This and many other big and small things is, I believe, where I get my Britishness from.

But what I also would like to say is, because I was born in the north-eastern corner of Ireland and I am living in a British state, doesn't mean that there isn't an Irish culture in Northern Ireland too, and that it has always been there.

There are many things which I hold dear which are Irish. For instance, I like Gaelic sports. Whenever on a Sunday afternoon there's Gaelic football on television I would watch it. I would obviously have more interest in the match if it was a team from Ulster, if it was Donegal, Tyrone or Derry, but that doesn't really matter, it's a great game. I also like Irish dancing and the Irish language. I suppose the Irish language somehow belongs to my cultural heritage, as I believe my ancestors, at least on my mother's side, at one time would have spoken the Gaelic language, as was, and to some degree still is, the practice among the people living in the Scottish Highlands.

I used to spend much of my holidays in the Republic of Ireland. I would go somewhere quiet and peaceful and picturesque, and there is a lot of places in the Republic of Ireland where you will find that. I usually go to Connemara or Cork. I try to avoid areas that are very Irish, maybe areas with a lot of Irish traditional music because often there are people, or 'Budweiser republicans' as I would call them, there that would know me and I wouldn't like spending my holiday being tortured by them. During all the time that I have spent in the

Republic I think I have had only one bad experience, and that one doesn't count. Ninety-nine out of a hundred people have been very nice and friendly to me. It is as many as that.

There might be prejudices against people from Northern Ireland in the Republic, but I have certainly not felt them. The reason for that might be that quite a lot of people in the Republic recognise what I and the party, the Progressive Unionist Party, are trying to do politically. The media in the Republic always gave us a fair crack of the whip, whereas it is not like that in the North because in Northern Ireland we have a unionist and a nationalist media, but mainly unionist and it tends to support mainstream unionism rather than radical thinkers like ourselves. In the Republic of Ireland people seem to like our radical thinking, they seem to think that they can do business with people like us rather than with mainstream unionists.

So I don't have a problem saying that I am British and telling you the reasons why I am British, and I can also say that I don't have a problem embracing those things that are Irish. I am not anti-Irish in any sense. There are Irish customs and traditions which I think are very good and that I think should be embraced by more people. I don't have a problem with those sort of things. There are things that are part of me that are Irish and I won't deny that. I have nothing to fear from Irish culture. The things that I fear are people and people's political ideologies.

What concerns me is that people have a republican ideology which is about blood sacrifice, it's about driving the British out of Ireland. I think the republicans or the nationalists are entitled to aspire to a united Ireland and they of course should be allowed to encourage people to actually work politically for a united Ireland. There is no fear and threat in that as long as they are trying to achieve it through a democratic process, but all this romantic notion about fighting with arms and bullets for a united Ireland, I don't agree with that and I will always stand up against it, because when people say 'Brits out' what they really are talking about driving out of Ireland is me and my friends and my people, and they always want to do it by physical force. People have to argue their corner, but they also have to recognise that the other people have a right as well. I have the right to call myself British; equally, I think that the people of the nationalist tradition in Northern Ireland have the right to call themselves Irish, and they don't necessarily have to recognise their Britishness.

There are some people who would say that Ireland should go back into the Commonwealth and that would be okay for me if it happened, but I don't think that the majority of the people in the Republic of Ireland would want to be in the Commonwealth or want to be united with Britain again, and for that reason I have no right to try and force my will on them. It is the same with Northern Ireland, and the fact is that almost all people, different parties and groupings, bar IRA and Sinn Féin, have recognised the principle of consent, which means that they will live and operate within the United Kingdom until the majority of the people of Northern Ireland says differently. The IRA and Sinn Féin have never, since 1921, accepted the border between the Republic of Ireland and Northern Ireland.

There are so many contradictions in this conflict, and there is so much hate and bitterness and sectarianism that we need to do away with before we can live together. It would be so much easier if it was just a question about making a deal on a piece of land.

For example, take when I was coming home from England on Sunday night, on the boat, and I was harangued by these two Manchester United fans. They were drunk and called me an 'Orange bastard' and said that they were Provos and that they were going to kill me and do this and that, and the sooner the Brits were out of Ireland the better. I just thought about the whole thing, them there shouting at me and wanting to get rid of the Brits, on their way back from supporting an English soccer team, a team that plays in an English city which the IRA blew up not that long ago! It is really sad. We seem to be so close to each other and at the same time so far far away. It is in many senses a very strange conflict.

But since the reality is as it is, in Northern Ireland people feel that they all the time have to prove their Britishness or their Irishness, that they have to fly their flag, and it is always in the face of adversity: 'Somebody else doesn't want me to fly my flag so I am going to do it!' The result is that the nationalist or Irish people in Northern Ireland, or however we want to describe them, are more Irish than the people in Cork or the people in Dublin, and the British in Northern Ireland are more British than the British in Kingsley. You will get people from both communities who say: 'There will be no dilution of our Irishness – or of our Britishness – and we are not going to let anybody tell us anything different.' Some people insist on seeing anything that is British as being wrong, and others anything that is Irish as being wrong.

I know people from republican families who aren't necessarily republicans, but their parents or brothers or sisters would be. They grew up in houses where British magazines weren't allowed in or where they wouldn't have been allowed to watch certain television programmes because they would have been seen as programmes spreading British propaganda. And on the other hand, in more recent years we have been able to get Radio Teilifís Éireann in Northern Ireland, and some people of the Protestant or unionist tradition would watch its programmes while others wouldn't. Some people watch it because they like to see the horse-racing or they like to see football or whatever RTE is bringing them, but other people would say, 'Oh, you can't watch television programmes from the Irish Republic. If you watch those maybe you will end up a united Irishman,' or something like that.

I am not really criticising people for these things because as reality stands I can understand them; I am only saying that this is how bogged down the situation is. There are very few things in Northern Ireland that you do in life that aren't segregated. Unless you go to a middle-class area there is very little likelihood of people socialising at all. Whenever you become of working age you can work with Catholics or Protestants, but that would be about it, that you are employed by the same firms. There is an almost total segregation of working-class people and it is the working-class people that has been standing at the front-line against each other during the conflict. People are born in different hospitals and they are buried in different graveyards. The whole education system is separate. If you are going to be a teacher and you are a Catholic, you are taught in a different training school than if you are a Protestant who is going to be a teacher. That is to be very general about it. There are opportunities for people to mix when it comes to both housing and education, but they are few and far between.

My son goes to an integrated school where he is taught together with Catholics and Protestants. He learns, which I didn't do when I went to school, about Gaelic sports and Irish history, as well as about British sports and British history. The reason why we decided to send him to an integrated school is so he can have Catholic friends, and I hope that he will find them. He certainly wouldn't hear any sectarian talk from me or from his mother if he one day said that he wanted to, say, marry a Catholic girl. As it is today, it would be very difficult for anybody in Northern Ireland to live in a mixed marriage, but we would of course wish them well and do all we can to support them. It's my son's decision at the end of the day what he wants to do with his life, and not mine. All I can do is to try and provide a good environment for him to grow up in and try to help him to be educated and open-minded.

What I believe both traditions or communities in Northern Ireland need to do is to wake up and realise that the culture on this island is a combination of both Irish and British cultures. People in Northern Ireland, nationalists and unionists, need to recognise that they couldn't have lived in this part of the island and not actually have been touched in some way either by British culture or Irish culture. When you live here you will always be influenced by the two cultures. Many people will refuse to recognise that and I think it is a shame that they actually do so, because you will find that they are the people who are either anti-British or anti-Irish, and this anti-Irishness and anti-Britishness is very dangerous because that engages people in sectarianism, which we need to do away with. We can't afford to have this constant antagonism about everything if we ever are going to live in harmony together.

When I say that I have an affinity with working-class people in England, it doesn't mean that I couldn't have an affinity with people on the Falls here in Belfast and in Derry, too, if I only was allowed to have that bond, as I believe I could have an affinity with people in the Republic. Obviously the Southerners are different culturally, as it happens, but I think cultures and people are changing and I am too, and that's good, that's how we go forward.

The roots and the history of this conflict are very complicated and very difficult to explain in a few sentences, but if you go back to before the establishment of Northern Ireland as a state you had the union with Great Britain, which was Ireland, England, Scotland and Wales. At the time there was a number of people in Ireland, people who were Irish, who wanted an Irish state independent of Britain. There were also a number of people, people like my grandfather, who wanted to remain part of the union with Great Britain. The outcome of the many negotiations that was going on was a deal made in 1921 that said that the six counties in the north-east of Ireland would remain part of the United Kingdom and the other twenty-six counties would stand alone as the Irish Free State. Some people were happy with the result and accepted it, others did not, and a civil war followed in the twenty-six counties.

Both states, both Northern Ireland and the Irish Free State, were far from perfect. In both states there was discrimination against the minority. In the Irish Free State it was against Protestants or the unionist minority, and in Northern Ireland it was against the Catholic Irish minority.

Eventually, in 1969 we had a civil rights campaign in Northern Ireland where people campaigned for equal rights for British citizens within Northern Ireland, that there should be one man one vote, fair housing and employment, and so on, and nobody can argue about that. These were very valid points: there definitely was discrimination going on in Northern Ireland.

I think one of the reasons the discrimination wasn't dealt with was because the republicans hijacked the civil rights movement, which was actually founded by Protestants at Queen's University. They hijacked it and turned it into a sectarian argument by saying it was only nationalists or republicans or Catholics who were suffering from a lack of civil rights, and a lot of people would still believe that that is the case today.

The truth is that the system in Northern Ireland was oppressive against Catholics, but it was oppressive against Protestants as well. It oppressed the Protestant working-class people. What the Protestant working class didn't realise at the time was that they were as badly off or almost as badly off as the Catholics.

Some unionist people said at the time that there was an ulterior motive behind the civil rights movement, that these people asking for British rights were really Irish republicans and that they weren't genuine about British rights for British people, that all they were interested in was overthrowing the state of Northern Ireland. The conflict escalated, we had street violence, and the Irish Republican Army and the Ulster Volunteer Force, which had been dormant during the sixties, sprung into life again, and other paramilitary organisations appeared as well. The British army was called in and we got what we now colloquially call 'the Troubles', which is basically the name for the armed conflict that has existed in Northern Ireland since 1969.

Some groups – the mill owners, the factory owners: the 'fur coat brigade', the people with the money – successfully got working-class Protestants to focus their interest on the constitutional issue, which is the issue which maintains our union, and they got them involved in sectarian hatred. They continuously fed the Protestant working-class with a rhetoric that said things like: 'You have to watch these Catholics because they are subversive and they are trying to bring the state down by attacking industry, and the trade unions are infiltrated by communists and communism is working hand in hand with Catholicism,' and so on. Of course, when you examined it, it was all nonsense. It was in the interests of these people to create division between the two traditions. They discriminated against Catholics in terms of work and they gave the Protestants the jobs at a very cheap rate.

I – and most people on the left of my party – would argue that for quite a number of years we were duped. If duped is the right word I am not sure, but we were always led to believe that we were well off and better off than the Catholics. Bernadette McAliskey, formerly known as Bernadette Devlin, who is a nationalist and who has been involved in the Troubles, has got a very nice description for what I have just tried to explain. She said at one time that the people of the Shankill, that were Protestant and unionist, were 'tuppence-ha'penny looking down on tuppence' – the people of the Falls who were Catholic and nationalist. So in other words she was saying that the difference between Protestants and Catholics in this country was worth a ha'penny.

Working-class Prods were second-class citizens and the Catholics third class. I remember Gusty Spence, who is like an elder statesmen in terms of loyalism and a mentor to me, relaying a story that I think says a lot. He once went into a betting-shop in the middle of Shankill Road, and there were these two men having an argument about who owned Australia. One of them was saying that we, in other words the British, owned Australia. The other said, 'Don't talk nonsense, we don't own Australia.' So when they saw Gusty one of them stopped the conversation and said, 'Gusty, you are an educated man, you have been all over the world fighting for the British. Tell us, who owns Australia? Don't we own it?'

Gusty said, 'We do, but look at yourself – you haven't even got an arse in your trousers and here you are talking about owning Australia!' What Gusty was saying was, it's okay having all this power and possessing all these countries around the world, but what does it mean for people like us? Nothing.

It's difficult to know what a solution to the conflict might be, because obviously anybody who is going to come up with a solution for Northern Ireland is going to come up with something that suits him and not necessarily a solution that suits the opposition or people from other parties. There are lots of different ideas around. The division between the traditions in Northern Ireland is not so clear-cut that 900,000 Protestant people want to stay in the United Kingdom and 600,000 Catholics want a united Ireland. Within the Protestant community you have people who would like to see an independent Ulster, you have people who would like to see full integration with Britain, you have people who want to see a devolved government in Northern Ireland with shared power across the parties. You also have people who would say that there should be a federal Ireland.

We in the PUP say that there is no reason why there can't be some sort of links, institutional or whatever, between Northern Ireland and the Republic of Ireland. We think there should be a relationship formed with the Republic of Ireland in the sense that we would look to people in the Republic to see how we could best co-operate to make this island better for everyone to live on.

We believe that we need to create a pluralist society in Northern Ireland, and we believe that that society has to be within the United Kingdom. For us to turn around and say that we should have something totally different, for example, that we should go outside the UK and have a united Ireland, that would be to completely give up our beliefs, and I think to ask that from us would be to ask too much.

But whatever the solution is, I don't think that anything can be imposed on either side in this conflict. What we in the PUP are saying is: 'Look, let's end this bloody conflict. Let's sit down and talk, let's find a way out of this. This is our solution. You tell us whether you can work with that, and if you can't then tell us what it is you want and we will tell you then if we will agree or not agree with you.' I think that we have to talk it out and we have to come to an agreement, and the only way that we are going to have peace in this country is when we find agreement among all the parties. We should all recognise that the Provos and Sinn Féin need to be at the table. Our party is looking forward to talking to Sinn Féin, but it has to be in the right atmosphere: it can't be when the IRA is blowing people up.

It was like lifting a weight off our shoulders when the IRA ceasefire came in 1994. It was a question of walking safely on the streets and feeling good. It was very encouraging for the future. When you looked at young children walking up and down the road in the centre of the city you felt, 'Maybe, just maybe this is it, that these kids will never see violence on the scale we have seen it.' All that has been shattered since the IRA took up the violent campaign again, but we still hang in and hope that the Provos will come to their senses. We will continue doing what we are doing, and that is to try and hold the loyalist ceasefire that we brokered in 1994.

What we have to do is to continue to work, to continue to give out messages and see what people go for and at the end of the day come up with solutions and see if people buy into them.

This whole process, as I suppose is the case with all peace processes, is about perseverance, it is about a battle of wits and a battle of wills. You just have to keep going. At the end of the day we will find a solution. Every time we have tried to find a solution we have failed, but I hope that the people that come after us will learn from the mistakes that have been made. I believe that the young people will change things. It may take another generation or two, but I think more and more of them are being disillusioned by what is going on in this country, and that more and more of them are recognising what needs to be done and sooner or later there will be a swell of young people who will start to move politically. My only concern would be that every time we fail in an attempt to find a solution we will go back to the armed struggle, and people will continue to die. I think that would be very sad.

Before I joined the Progressive Unionist Party I was in prison. I spent sixteen years in prison from 1974 until 1990 for murder. While I was in prison I did quite a lot of work in the background, trying to write policies for the party and trying to encourage people that the best way forward was through political dialogue rather than through acts of political violence.

To go from a violent armed struggle to fight for my beliefs in a democratic way wasn't something that came to me like a flash of lightning; it was something that I learned and understood over the years. It wasn't only me; it was a world-wide trend. In the sixties you had the student demonstrations for different causes, then in the seventies you moved towards international terrorism in pursuit of political aims, and again in the eighties it changed when people moved more towards negotiated settlements. There were cases around the world where you had people who had spent a lot of time in prison and who had

67

become statesmen in their own countries and who had been recognised as trying to bring about peace. I, too, felt that terrorism had burnt itself out, that it had been tried here for a number of years but that it hadn't worked. I felt that the best way to deal with our problem in Northern Ireland was to get people to actually start talking about the problems and to start negotiating with each other.

I don't think that I have contributed that much to finding a solution to the Northern Ireland conflict, but I feel that people like myself who have been to prison probably would be seen by many, and especially by young people, as some kind of a hero, and that we should take that opportunity and try to give leadership to people and to get them to understand that there is more power in negotiating than in the gun.

A problem is that the history of the conflict is so long and embittered, so many people have lost their lives and so many people are holding grudges from the past, at the same time as there is a great fear about what the future holds. It is quite difficult for many people to see their way through the whole thing – but not for everybody! There are people, people from both traditions, that have been trying to do things and that have been doing things together over the divide even during the worst times of the Troubles. If they hadn't done that, Northern Ireland would have been a much worse place to live in and there would have been many more people dead. A lot of people have worked very hard over the last twenty-seven years in trying to achieve peace, and also trying to achieve some kind of common understanding between the different traditions. I think quite a lot of people have been touched by that work, and you would see that as a result people probably have been prevented from taking part either in the violence or supporting the war efforts in both communities. This absolutely important ground-work that we so seldom hear or read about in the media has to continue. There is no point leaving it all up to the politicians. The communities have to work together and they have to be sure that they build a base at ground-level, so that whatever is implemented or whatever is proposed by politicians can work, and people feel part of it.

I think there has to be a recognition that there are many things in Northern Ireland that are of common interest, like unemployment, health conditions, education, housing, civil rights. All these are the big important issues that are facing us all the time, whether there is a conflict or not, and we can't allow them to wait until we find an overall solution, because if we do then we will have nothing to find a solution for.

Seán Ó Siadhail

ABOUT TWO AND a half thousand years ago the Celts were spread right through Europe. They were very strong and dominated big parts of the Continent. Their language was spoken in most parts of central, western and southern Europe. Then the Romans came, the Celts lost power and were more or less assimilated into other cultures on the Continent. In Britain and in Ireland, they survived a bit longer.

Within the Celtic language there were different groups. In the Breton group you had for example Cornish, which is a completely dead language today. And you had Cymric, which became the Welsh language. In the Gaelic group you had Manx spoken on the Isle of Man, but that is also an almost dead language, and you had Gaelic in Scotland, which is very close to Irish. In fact, I think the Scottish Gaels were a tribe that emigrated from Ulster, and that Gaelic in the beginning was a dialect of Irish. Gaelic is still alive, but I believe it is to a large degree spoken by old people. The Welsh language seems in contrast to be fully alive. I think that's a result of the old structure of Welsh society. They still have their mines of tin and coal that they have had since maybe the twelfth century. What I am saying is that the circumstances for their language haven't really changed, and they still have a use for it in their society.

I believe the Irish language came into Ireland about 2,000 years ago. It is the oldest written language in Europe, or could Italian be it, if one sees Italian as a direct descendant from

Latin? I don't really know, I am not an expert on this.

I wouldn't be able at all to read the Old Irish, except maybe for a few words that I might recognise. There are some reasonably accessible texts from the fourteenth and fifteenth centuries. You have some poems and love songs – for example, the romance of Diarmaid and Gráinne – but if you go further back it is almost like a different language. Dallan Forgaill's elegy about the dead saint from the end of the sixth century would be like double Dutch to me.

Irish has, at least in the past 200 years, been a story of impoverishment. Before that it was a strong language in line with many other European languages. Irish is said by many people to be a rich and beautiful language. I have never thought about it. Maybe it was rich and beautiful once upon a time, at least compared to today's modern Irish, which is certainly very deprived. You know the way a language generates. Say you have new trades in a country, to cope with them you will have to find a language that suits them and the new situation you are living in and have to deal with. These new activities will feed the language and make it bigger. The language of a country can be as big and deep and full of meaning as the real life of that country. This 'natural growth' of a language gets into serious problems when there are two languages to be dealt with. Bilingualism is a problem; at least from the point of view of language, it is not good. What I see happening in Ireland and with the Irish language is that the whole logical syntax of Irish is being taken over by the English syntax. Many Irish speakers of today are, at least to a degree, speaking Irish words, but the English syntax is stronger in their mind, so they will invent words or sentences in Irish to make the Irish understandable to themselves. I'll give you an example: 'I hope' is *Tá súil agam* in Irish. There is no

'I' in Irish in that context, but because the English begins with an 'I', a lot of Irish speakers would start the sentence with '*tá mé*' which means 'I am', and then follow the English syntax and say: '*Tá mé ag hópáil.*' Now, the word 'hópáil' doesn't exist in Irish, nor in English. It is some kind of Irish-English.

In one way it is quite a strong sign in a language to be able to renew itself in that way. In another it basically means that to survive in a bilingual situation one language has to copy the other, structure- and syntax-wise. The effect is that the stronger will form the weaker. That is no harm in one way, but if you are going to end up with a new language, or more likely, a kind of a patois that an Irish speaker wouldn't understand in fifty years time, then it is maybe not so positive.

During the earlier part of this century the majority of Irish speakers would have been poor small farmers and fishermen, and they would have been monoglots. Irish was a language which was very close to nature. The traditional activities that fed the language have maybe not died off, but changed dramatically, and the change has been all in English.

My mother tells a story about an older brother of mine, who died very young. When my father went to baptise my brother – he wanted to baptise him as Liam, which is the Irish name for the English William – some old friends of my mother said: 'That boy will never get a job in Derry with an Irish name like that.' The tendency was to baptise your child one way, the British way, and keep your own version privately. That was common throughout Ireland and not only in the North. It wasn't that the Irish language was forbidden; it just didn't get you anywhere. You had to speak English to get on in society. Obviously that didn't concern the farmer or the fisherman who organised his own way of living. That is also why Irish has persisted in these

73

groups. But for, say, the middle class, the Irish language was a no-go area. A vital group of Irish speakers was lost through this cultural ghettoisation. The intellectual life of the Irish language kind of died off. People kept speaking the language, but for a long time it wasn't taught, and it stopped developing.

That is a part of the history that has created today's poor situation for the Irish language. You have books in Irish, but you don't have the equivalent of what is available in English. You have some poetry, some fiction, some journalism, but it is very limited. All the hobbies, for example, are English dominated. And you have nothing of daily newspapers, fashion magazines, and, for example, if you're looking for information on say Freud, you'll have to go to English.

Still, it's not really a question of words that is lacking in Irish. There are enough of them, at least to start with. There is an official dictionary committee that produces words – but very few people use them, or know how to use them. The Irish of today is still very rural, which is not the case for the rest of the society, which has become very urban. It is almost like as if Irish belongs to a completely different society.

Ireland has not totally lost the Irish language. Many people would be able to read Irish, at least in a passable way, but very few could speak it, or would speak it. It depends on where the person stands. If you have no use for Irish, if you have no contact with the language, then you will have no interest in it, and it will be dead, or dying. There are a lot of Irish people in that situation.

Up until the first half of this century, there were pockets of Irish-speakers all over Ireland. A statistic from the thirties shows half a million *Gaeilgeoirí* at the time, to use a tainted word. I say tainted, because if you call somebody a *'Gaeilgeoir'* today, it also suggests that somebody is ultra-conservative and ultra-Catholic. It's a label. On a different level, it suggests someone who is fanatically interested in pushing Irish down other people's throats, with little or no regard for cultural or social realities.

Nowadays there are basically only parts of the west and south-west of Ireland, and of course the north-west, where Irish is still alive. Altogether there would be about 100,000, or fewer, people in the country that speak the language. We can maybe see a little revival in the last few years through a middle class that looks for Irish for their children, but overall it doesn't look too positive.. I hope I am not painting an unfair and unduly negative picture. Maybe *Teilifís na Gaeilge*, the new Irish-language TV station, will make an encouraging contribution?

Personally I see that there are two alternatives. Either you decide that the language can't come back, or that you don't care, or else you make a serious attempt to try to revive it. The problem for a lot of Irish people is that they are caught in between the two. They are claiming that they want to try to get the language back, but they are not doing anything about it. It demands a lot of effort to chose an extra language. I think, in life, if things are going to survive people have to want them strongly enough. As it is at the moment in Ireland, as regards the Irish language, we are in a kind of a limbo situation. It is not going really anywhere, except, I suppose, down. There is no real push in society for a revival of the language. The different governments that we have talk about the Irish language and the importance of the Irish language, but very little is actually done about or for it. I would obviously prefer if the politicians took this subject more seriously, instead of making half-attempts, pretending to be interested. In order for a language to survive, or to be revived, it is not enough to write it into the Constitution as having equal status with English, or to create a law that makes it compulsory in schools. Patrick Pearse, one of the leaders of the Easter Rising in Dublin in 1916, at the time attacked the establishment for this business he called 'the murder machine'. He meant by that the way the English educational system was pushed down the throats of kids that didn't even speak English. The irony is that it has almost gone the opposite way now. Today compulsory Irish is stuffed into kids that know only English and can see no reason why they should learn Irish.

I suppose my interest in Irish has a certain political or historical element to it. I live in the Republic, but I am originally from Derry, or from Londonderry, as I presume people informed by British news agencies would call it. Sometimes I think it shows a certain international ignorance to call Derry 'Londonderry', but, I suppose, at home it's a badge to say Derry or Londonderry, whilst in other countries it would only be a way for people to locate themselves geographically. Still, it is not without a certain importance. It is a bit like saying 'Gaelic' instead of 'Irish'. There would only be British, West Brits and foreigners that would say 'Gaelic' instead of Irish. What you say has, of course, its political implications. I wouldn't, for example, say 'Northern Ireland' about the North. If I ever use it I have been very commendably ecumenical, but it tends to stick in my craw. I call it the Six Counties. The reasons for that are political.

Once when I was in Portugal I happened to see a computer game. The manufacturers had taken away the six counties in the North as if they didn't belong to Ireland. It was as if they were an island in themselves. No, I said, this is not right, I am from the North and I am Irish. Obviously at one level it is harmless, but on another it dispossesses you. Somebody somewhere had made a political decision to portray the North that way, a way

76

Seán Ó Siadhail

that was not true for me. Through the years there have been too
many things like that concerning the North to feel relaxed and
happy about it. When I was growing up in Derry and was
watching the weather forecast on UTV or BBC, they would
show you a map of the North, but again as if it was an island on
its own in the middle of the sea with no other Ireland attached.
It gave a really bad feeling. Today, though, they would show the
rest of Ireland too.

My dad was born in Ulster. He would have been in what you
might call the old IRA. That is in the forties. The IRA wasn't a
very effective movement at that time, but what I want to say is
that my father was political. He never accepted that the Six
Counties in the North should belong to Great Britain.

My father taught me Irish at home. In a sense I think the Irish
language for my dad was a sort of present, a heritage to hand
over to me and my brothers who grew up in the sixties and
seventies, instead of passing on a kind of a sub-political role. He
was not interested in seeing us following the same political path
that he had done, because he saw no future for us in it. You
know, at the time there was a lot of internment in the North.
People were put in prisons left, right and centre by the British.
My dad didn't want that happening to us. I think it was an
alternative for him to give us Irish. You can see it as a sort of
residual resistance to the British occupation. I mean like,
English is the language that we feel isn't really ours. It's called
English, which in itself creates a problem directly from the
beginning. For me English in a sense is the language of the con-
queror, whereas I and the Irish belong to the conquered. Now,
you could probably overstate that and make a big thing of it if
you like to, but it isn't. It is not as if I go around hating the
English language and the English people. It is more a kind of a

77

consciousness that history somehow has played a dirty trick on us, an awareness that we in a sense were forced to drop our language. Of course, in another sense, the Irish people themselves decided to drop their language, but that was because a society had been created that had no place for that language, and the Irish people hadn't created that society themselves. For me to try to keep Irish alive is in a way to say, excuse me, fuck history! In that the Irish language is alive today, there is a feeling that we have survived despite all the oppression and the bad things that have happened to us in our history. I believe there is an element of retaining or regaining an identity in that. We did what we had to to survive. Now we try to regain what we had to abandon. Or, at the very least, to come to terms with the reality that some things cannot be regained! It is a process that is not finished, maybe not even really started. Maybe it is something we Irish have to make ourselves more conscious about.

I suppose I could see myself as somebody trying to foster a link with the past, for Ireland, and for myself. If my children decide that I was mistaken, and that they don't want to keep the Irish language up, then that is their decision. I don't really have any vision of the way I would like to have Ireland in a hundred years time. I am merely making the Irish language a part of my present reality, and I try to nurture that language as much and as well as I can.

Noreen Byrne

I CAN HARDLY BELIEVE the change that has taken place in this country in my adult life. There has certainly been a massive change in twenty-five years in Ireland in relation to women's rights, and especially in the last ten years. It is almost as if I have been living in two very different eras.

To describe this change a bit, and to speak very personally, when I was a young woman, and I am not that old, there was no way you were not going to be a virgin when you got married. You knew you couldn't have sex, because if you had sex you would get pregnant. That was it. And if you got pregnant outside marriage, had an unwanted pregnancy, you were in for serious trouble. The sanction was that you had to get out. If you lived in the countryside, you could maybe move to Dublin; if not, you moved to England. I don't know if you, coming from another culture, can understand what that means, what that feels like, when you have to leave your family and vanish? Personally I know many many women of my age who got pregnant and went to England and gave their children up for adoption. And then, if and when they came back, they had to carry on as if nothing had happened. Until twenty years ago, 80 per cent of babies born outside marriage in Ireland were adopted. Listen, up until 1987 all children born outside marriage were called 'illegitimate'. Almost like 'bastards', isn't it? There was no sense at all that you could rear a child on your own. Many of these women are married now and have other children. Imagine to have to live with that and never be able to speak about it! It must be very painful and difficult.

At that time, in the sixties and seventies, there was a very strong message that you had to get married and have children. I was in my early twenties at the end of the sixties. I was married and had two children. Then I started to take the pill. That was a really terrible thing to do then. No one else that I knew did it. They were all scared of what the priest would say in confession. Contraceptives were not legal at the time. I could only get the pill because my husband worked in Guinness's and they had their own medical department and the doctor was a Protestant. He gave me the pill with a wink 'to control my menstrual cycle'.

It was only in the seventies that women in Ireland stopped going to the church for a cleansing ceremony six weeks after they had their babies. You know, the priest blessed the woman and prayed for her. I let that ceremony happen to me with my first child, but not with the second. There was a huge row about it in my family, even if my family wasn't religious. Everybody was upset; my mother was crying. Religious behaviour was very deep rooted in the Irish person whether that person was a believer or not. The whole society was totally imbued with the Catholic ethos. To be Irish was to be Catholic, and it still is to a certain degree. I think it is a kind of an emotionally held notion. It is something very deep in the identity of the Irish person.

Ireland has been a very homogeneous society in cultural and religious terms. Until recently, something like 90 per cent of the population were Catholic churchgoers. You can imagine how that cultural homogeneity created a sense of, oh, yes, we should have these things, or this is how it should be. It was a very authoritarian society. Children had no rights; women had no rights. For example, until 1973, women that worked in the public service had to leave when they got married. That was what was called the 'marriage bar'. There were some exclusions, like teachers and nurses, but in general married women were prevented from working in the civil service. That was the way it was. In all, there were very few women in the labour market. It is really only in the last decade that that has started to change, and still, we are far away from the employment level of say Scandinavian women. In Ireland, women's place has very much been seen as being within the home.

Our Constitution was written by Eamon de Valera and his men in 1937. De Valera is like a hero, or a saint even, in our society. In the twenties, when the country was divided and Northern Ireland was created, de Valera took the anti-British and the republican line. When the Civil War was over, he and his party, Fianna Fáil, became very popular in politics, and have remained so into the eighties when serious changes started to be demanded in society. Fianna Fáil were conservative and very close to the Church. In fact, basically every political party at the time recognised the Church's authority. As soon as the Civil War was over and the British had lost their power, the Church moved in, and gradually it had gotten an increasing power over the affairs of the state and it became a very effective arbiter of social legislation. It was therefore seen as nothing strange when de Valera visited the Archbishop of Dublin with a draft of the Constitution before he brought it to the parliament. In pre-independent Ireland, divorce had been legally allowed, even if very difficult to obtain, as had contraceptives and information concerning birth control. The Constitution banned these rights, and a tremendous censorship of books and films was introduced. Such a thing as publishing or distributing literature advocating birth control became a criminal offence.

There was a campaign against the Constitution by women's groups, for example, from some of the groups that had been involved in the suffrage movement of 1922, but I am sure that they were seen as complete freaks. De Valera's own vision as regards women was that he wanted an Ireland where you would have 'maidens dancing at the crossroads'. The Constitution makes a very clear statement about the role of women. For example, it says something like, and I am paraphrasing it, that women shall not be obliged by economic necessity to work outside the home to the neglect of their home duties. There is also another clause which says that the state pledges to protect the family, which is based on marriage, to protect it against any kind of attack or however they now express it. So, you see, the Constitution is very traditional and conservative about what constitutes a family, and about the notion of the role of women in Irish society. In the social welfare code, women are treated as dependent on men.

Take an example from practical life: say that a woman is married to a man that is unemployed. Okay? He gets unemployment benefit in his name, for himself, for her and the children, but the benefit that he gets for her isn't equal to the amount that he gets for himself. It is three-fifths of the full benefit. It is described in this way using this language: a married man will get the Adult Personal Allowance, but the wife will get the Adult Dependant's Allowance. Now, say it is a difficult marriage and the man is keeping all the money, and drinking or gambling it away or whatever, then the woman has to apply to the Social Welfare to get her portion, and whatever happens he will still get his allowance, plus half the children's. The wife gets hers – that is, the three-fifths of the full benefit – plus half of the children's. This is completely crazy. It is pragmatism gone mad. The whole concept of dependency is just incredible. And there seem to be no changes on the way.

There are huge battles to be fought if we want equality between the sexes, and resistance to it is strong. While the conservative parties, forced by the voters, have been somehow pushing forward in terms of progressive policies, very right-wing, very religious fundamentalist political groups are emerging. They are an alliance between, if you like, ordinary people on the ground and academics and university people, and probably Church people, but you never know for certain about them as they usually work in secrecy. These different groups have names like Family Solidarity, The People of Ireland, Youth Defence, and you also have the American group Human Life International, and others. They are very vocal and vociferous.

There is a contradiction in Irish society about the role of women. On one hand, many women, and especially the younger women in their twenties, are pushing for their rights and they assume that they have rights, but when they come into conflict with the state, or sometimes in employment issues, then they realise that things are not as they seem to be. What happens is, you get so far, and then it is like the door closes. The Constitution is the legal framework against which all these different activities are happening. It is a very confining and rigid document to work with, and there is no consensus in sight about changing it either. There is a lot of tinkering and playing around with it, but attitudes to women are still very conditional. Yes, I think conditional is the word I would use, highly conditional. Okay, we, the people, the society, are prepared to give women their rights in a piecemeal fashion, but we are not prepared to look at the concepts about women in the Constitution, and what we as a society want to say about those concepts.

In Ireland you can see women everywhere in society. They are very visible – to a certain point. After that, there are only black suits and ties. Men on an individual basis, particularly younger men, are more open today to sharing power and to sharing responsibilities and the workload in the home than they were before, but at a broader level in society, sexism is extremely ingrained. Men seem to find it really hard to accept women as equal partners.

That we have got a woman like Mary Robinson as president first of all sends a very clear signal to society about how it sees itself, but it is also sending a very clear message to the Church and to women in general. It has given many women a tremendous boost, not simply because Mary Robinson is a woman – we could have got someone like Thatcher – but because she has a track record of women's issues she fought as a lawyer. She fought all that when I was a young woman. And you have to remember that there hadn't been a single woman serving as a government minister in Ireland between 1922 and 1979.

Don't forget that Irish women were educated by the Catholic Church to be 'good girls'. The image of Our Lady was our role model. Our Lady was a very passive woman who obeyed her son and her husband, and that was what we Irish women also were supposed to do. We were not to be angry, or at least not to show our anger. I think that many Irish women, because of that, still find it very hard to push themselves forward. I can see that women's groups often try to find ways to campaign on issues without rocking the boat.

Also bear in mind that Ireland is a very small society with a very strong social pressure and control. Let us say that you take a public stand on the abortion issue. I mean, everybody will know it instantly, and they will nod to each other and say, 'You know, she is an abortionist.' It makes it really hard to push forward.

And despite this, there is a huge development today where women are ready, and not afraid any more, to stand up for their views and needs. That absence of fear is what is driving things forward, that sense of real citizenship: 'This is my country. I live here, and I want to have a say in my life.' Women are becoming much more active in terms of how they vote. Today they vote on the basis of their own realities, and not because their family traditionally voted this way or that. Women, and maybe I should say people in general, are now looking for concrete reasons why they should vote for a particular party. 'What has this party to offer me?' they ask.

When we had the abortion referendum in 1983, people had to listen to an unbelievable amount of abuse from many priests and bishops about the issue. They would say things like, 'Women that have abortions are murderers.' Very few people dared to walk out of the church then. Today I think we are in a very different situation. People would just stand up and either leave the church, or say straight to the priest that they don't like that way of talking. Women are not afraid any more. They are fed up with all this simplistic talk, and they won't let themselves be intimidated any longer.

Today there are about 3,000 women's groups around the country. For a decade there has been a glorious outburst of activity by women for their rights. I am very hopeful about the future for women in Ireland. The organisation that I am chairperson of, the National Women's Council of Ireland, incorporates everything from rather conservative country women to lesbian extremist feminists. The women's movement in Ireland hasn't split up as it has in so many other countries. I suppose we couldn't afford to do that as our problems are so big and difficult. Today there is a sense that there is a collective voice for women in our country. The movement is in a very healthy state. It has become a hugely important pressure group. In the past an organisation like this would have been sidelined. Today nobody can ignore us. Women are not difficult to get to come out on the streets any more.

The result of this whole movement for women's rights has been tremendous. Ten years ago I was in a group of women that set up a centre for lone parents. At the time a centre like that was highly innovative, almost dangerous to set up. It was very new and very provocative for many people, men and women, and for certain established institutions, that women were speaking about their own matters on their own behalf. In ten years we have got many other groups like that. Now, we have, for example, a rape crisis centre in basically every town around Ireland, and finally, after a lot of struggle, we got the right to divorce. We have also got contraception again. Today you find condoms available in supermarkets and pubs. We have not got a right to abortion but we have got the right to information on abortion, a right which I am sure that many people from other countries would find slightly strange. It is crazy, but it is a typical Irish solution to a problem. It is a kind of a close-your-eyes attitude. In the Constitution we have a ban on abortion, but at the same time we now have the right for women to get information about abortion in other countries and to travel abroad to have an abortion. So, as long as it happens elsewhere it is okay. There are thousands of Irish women and girls travelling to England every year to have an abortion. Somewhere in my mind I keep comparing that to the situation of the women that were forced to run away to England twenty years ago to put their 'illegitimate children' up for adoption. It is the same kind of rejection of people, of women, and of reality that exists in society.

There are many contradictions in Irish society. The Constitution says that the family is the basis of our society, and yet 30 per cent of all births are outside marriage. And the family is supposed to be based on marriage, while in reality many young men and women live together without being married. So, in people's daily life they are living in a different way from the way people feel it should be, or the way the Constitution says it should be. It is really an unhealthy climate. You are, as an individual, pulled strongly on one hand by the old traditions and values, and on the other by the possibilities of development and the values of a modern society. Irish society is split on many questions, but people are split, too. I think it can be very difficult and frustrating for many people to live in Ireland today. For others it is a fascinating time of change.

Gráinne Daly

Yes, I WOULD DEFINITELY like to stay in this area. I simply love it around here. It is not just the beautiful landscape with the sea and the mountains and the bogs, it is the people as well. You know everybody here. You mightn't know them by name, but you know everybody to see and everybody still waves at each other. People usually think the communities are too small over here, that everybody knows everybody's business, but I think that's great. If everyone knows your business you have nothing to hide from anybody.

When I say I want to stay in the area I don't mean in County Clare; it's north Clare I want to settle in. There is no way I would settle, say, ten miles down the road towards Milltown, or five miles to Inagh or up towards Lisdoonvarna. It is just this one tiny little area where we are now that I would like to settle in.

I think that we are lucky, you can have a nice relaxing life when you live here. You can get up at ten o'clock in the morning or whenever you like, there is no one pointing a finger at you saying you should be up at six o'clock. Around here you can do basically almost anything you want.

I would love to live in a small little cottage, a small little farm with twenty acres where we – I hope to get married one day – could have a little bit of everything, a couple of horses, a few hens, geese and a garden. I would like to one day be able to open up a home-produce store in Ennistymon where I could sell what we produce on our farm.

Matchmaking is something I would like to do in my spare time. For a couple of years I have been helping my dad with it but I would like one day, if he ever retires or gets too old for it or whatever, to actually take it over and keep it going, but I will always do it with him as long as he is interested. There's no rush anyway, I am only twenty and I have an awful lot to learn yet to be able to matchmake on my own. I have to get better with people, not to be as rash. I think when you are younger and you meet people you tend to straightaway put them into certain categories, which is wrong, because when you meet people for the first time they are usually only showing you what they want to show you. I suppose I am still a bit naïve in ways. I have often said to Dad when he has been talking about people that he has been thinking about matching together: 'You can't do that, that is not going to work out at all. Sure, she doesn't know anything about this, or, she is from the city and what would she be doing up here on a farm?' I have often been wrong.

I watch Dad when he is meeting people. He seems to give off an air to people that makes them feel that he sees straight through them, that he knows and understands them, and that makes them calm down and it brings out their genuine side. That's how I would like to be with people.

I wouldn't like to get into matchmaking on a big scale with two, three hundred people on the books. It's not something that I am planning to make a living out of, but I would like to get into a situation where I could do it just like a hobby.

I believe that there is always going to be a need for a matchmaker in the area. People at my age, they will need matchmakers as well no matter what they think, and there are still an awful lot of single men in the area, many more than single women, and there is a lot of young men. In general I think there

are at least two men for every woman on this side of the River
Shannon. If you walk into a pub on a week-night the chances
are that there will be mainly fellows in there and very few girls,
except for during the summer of course when there is a lot of
tourists around.

Many of the men around here are used to meeting girls in the
summer, for two, three weeks before the girls head off again
and other girls come in for two, three weeks and so on, and that
might be fine for a while, but then when they get to a certain
age they find that they get tired of the girls heading off and they
want to settle down. There are a lot of men over the thirty mark
here who aren't married and who are looking for women.

But it is not just for the locals that I would love to matchmake; it's about people. I am a people's person. I love people
and I know that people need people. Even on the phone talking
to people you feel the want that they have and the need that
they have to meet somebody, but for some reason or other they
can't or don't succeed on their own.

Computer-dating is supposed to be very popular these days
but I think a big difference is that with computer-dating you are
simply just dating, whereas with a matchmaker you are looking
for a potential lifelong partner.

It is not to get people married that is important to me, it's to
lead people to each other. A lot of the time you would introduce people and you would never find out whether they are getting married or not. I think that it is great when they do get
married, but it is not really important, it's that they find someone to share and build a life together with that is important. In
your matchmaker's mind, you don't introduce them to a fort-
night's relationship, you introduce them for a potential lifelong
relationship, and that's why you have to be so cautious. It's not

a pleasure game, it's serious business, it's about deep feelings and needs in people. It's something that you have to handle with care and respect.

Many Irish people, perhaps especially among the rural population, are still very old-fashioned in ways. There is still a lot of people that wouldn't, for example, have sex before they get married and they would like to meet someone who is the same. Of course they wouldn't trust the ads in the papers, and rightly so. I don't know anybody or I have never heard about anybody that has ever met a partner for life through a newspaper, through the Lonely Hearts column or whatever it can be. These ads seem to be so sex-orientated. It must be very difficult to know if someone wants you only for a night or for a longer relationship. A personal contact with a matchmaker is different, it's on another level of seriousness.

There are so many different people that need a matchmaker. I remember going through Dad's books with him one day and I found a twenty-one-year-old fellow there. I got the shock of my life and said, 'What is he doing in the books? He is young enough to be able to find someone himself.' And I just realised then that it is not only old people that are shy. There are so many people that are simply too shy to meet anybody by themselves. I personally love country fellows who are shy. There is a lot of them that are so shy that if I walked up to them they wouldn't talk to me, they wouldn't know what to say, they have never been around women and they would just start blushing.

When I say I love country fellows who are shy I think I should say that I love Irish country people in general. They have often got a great kind of simplicity, they think of things in a simple sort of way. But they are not simple! It is something nice about them, they are so innocent in certain ways, and yet they aren't in other ways. I can understand why they seem to be so attractive to so many foreign women, American women, for example. Many of the country men around here have still got a lot of culture in them. Many of them can still speak Irish to a degree and they can sing every tune that you have in the country, they know the step-dance or the Irish dance, they know music and you would be astonished at how many good storytellers there are around. These men have got the old stories from their grandparents and grand-aunts and grand-uncles and they can be really interesting and fun. They would be very different from the ordinary money-and-career-concentrated western man.

I also particularly love old people. Men in their sixties and seventies seem to be very soft and gentle towards women and often more respectful than younger men. I am not against equality between the sexes, not at all, of course we should have that, but I still like it when a man holds open the door to a woman, and elder men seem to know how to treat women in that sense.

There are a good few older people who contact us in the hope that we can help them to find a partner. A couple of years ago there was this man who kept phoning and asking Dad to look out for a woman for him. The man was close to eighty and Dad tried to gently put him off the thought of getting married, but the man kept insisting. His mother with whom he had lived his whole life had died, and now he wanted to do what he had always dreamed of: to get a woman. Dad thought, 'Fair play to him.' In this business you give everyone the benefit of the doubt. You never turn around to somebody and say, 'There is no hope for you.' Unless you have introduced them once or twice or even a third time and you know in your heart and in your head and in your soul that there is no hope for this man to meet somebody, at least not through you, then you might in some sensitive way make that clear to him. It isn't easy to find some-one for everybody, and the more they have in their baggage the more difficult it gets.

This old man said, like most people that contact us would say, that he just wanted to meet somebody that was kind and decent. Dad kept the man in his mind and finally he got in contact with this thirty-seven-year-old widow that a few, five, seven years earlier had lost her husband in an accident when he was milking the cows. She had contacted Dad and had said she would like to meet a man, that the age wasn't important, the most important was that he didn't think about material things all the time and that he was fit to move around. Dad talked to her about the old man and she agreed to meet him, and they met and it worked out well, they got married and still are, and when Dad met the woman the other day she said she was completely satisfied, in all regards. The old man's cousin, who was seventy-seven and who was best man at the wedding, phoned Dad a couple of weeks after the wedding and asked if he couldn't find a woman for him, too.

I also feel very strongly about the small farmers with thirty, forty acres of land and who are in their fifties, sixties and not married. It is really sad when you look at them and they have no children to hand the farm down to, especially when you know what the land has meant to them. What happens to the farm when the owner is dead is that it is either eaten up by the big farmer or else you get foreigners that come in and buy up the land and maybe give the land over to forestry, which I think is an awful shame. It is terrible actually, and if I could find partners for these bachelor farmers it would make me very happy. That would be my way of defending life in rural communities and trying to stop the depopulation of the countryside.

In all fairness, there is a certain amount of strangers that have moved into houses when they for one reason or another have become vacant, especially people involved in crafts and art, and I think they have added something new to our community, they have brought new ideas and new attitudes, and that is vitally important to us as it keeps our small communities and our countryside alive.

There is also this agency set up to help families to move from places like Tallaght or Ballymun or other suburbs of Dublin to depopulated areas in County Clare. They are given a house and a bit of land. They are well screened before they are accepted for the move, and only people are selected who would be adaptable to the life here and who could add something to the life of the place they go to. This has been quite successful, it has made it possible to keep schools open, which is good since small schools are always endangered in areas like this. If the population goes down the school will close, and when a community loses its school it loses a certain amount of its identity and its energy. It can be quite tragic for a community.

There is a lot of people moving away from here but there is a lot of people wanting to come back as well. Many women that moved to the cities when they were young would love to settle in the country and meet a farmer. You get a lot of country women that are nurses in the cities and who just want to move back out into the country again. The towns or cities seem to suffocate them after a while. A lot of the women from the cities would be women that have kids, but their husbands might have left them or they might have left their husbands.

I was in London for a couple of weeks not long ago and I went into an Irish centre where I met a lot of Irish people, and many of them would love to come back to Ireland. One way of getting them back is to introduce them to people over here.

We usually don't need to advertise to get people. Dad is so well-known – he has been on television and in newspapers and magazines – that we usually get enough people interested through that. It's word of mouth really. The odd time if the numbers get low in the books, or say if you are short of women, you might just do an advertisement in a local newspaper, like the *Kerryman* or whatever. Usually we write something like: 'Renowned matchmaker Willie Daly looking for ladies.'

It often depends on the season how many we have in our books. Sometimes we have a lot. Say if an article is published about Dad in a foreign paper, two weeks later you will have maybe fifteen letters from that country. We constantly get new letters coming in, and then we have got our old stock that we are still dealing with. At the moment we have got about maybe fifty, sixty people, roughly half women, half men. They are from all walks of life, but there would be a lot of farmers or people with a farming background. I suppose matchmaking is more of a traditional thing with farmers.

When you are doing this type of work you are basically working all the time. You can't really sit down and take an hour in the evening and do your matchmaking job: you pick it up all day long. If I am working behind the counter in Dad's pub and some fellow walks in, and even if he doesn't come to you to look for a match to be made, you will be trying to suss out if he is on his own and what type of person he is, and before the day is over you will know if he would mind if someone was introduced to him or not. Or if Dad and I get out together for a night and we are talking to people, then on the way home we would most probably be discussing them and thinking about if we have anybody that they could match. They mightn't have said anything at all to us but you know yourself that they would love to meet a woman. They would get mad if they knew what we are saying about them.

You couldn't matchmake just around here nowadays. If a neighbour comes up to you, or you for some reason realise that he wants to meet somebody, the chances are that you will have to introduce him to somebody in another county, in Galway, Kerry, Limerick, or to somebody from abroad.

The matchmaking is another business today than it was earlier in history. If you think about fifty or a hundred years ago, a matchmaker was in his area alone and that was it. He knew everybody. At that time a matchmaker maybe only had to ride ten miles down the road to talk to somebody; nowadays you get people contacting you from all over Ireland and from all over the world. It would be very difficult to matchmake without the phone today, although we do a lot of business in Lisdoonvarna in September when the yearly matchmaking festival is on.

Lisdoonvarna has been famous as a matchmaking town for many many years. It's a spa town. People would have gone there on their holidays after the harvesting was over, when the hay and the turf was brought in, when all the important things for a farmer were done. It started out where landlords and land-owners would be looking for somebody that they could swap sons and daughters with. Then it became popular for working-class people as well to go there to meet up – and today it is a huge matchmaking festival with a very high success rate. There is a lot of bed-hopping going on but there is also a lot of serious matchmaking being done. Dad has matched many many people there. The minute people see him they are up straightaway to put their names down into the book.

It is a bit scary the first time you go there, when you see all these single men and all these single women walking around. It was a complete shock to me when I saw these aged American women, who have had multiple plastic surgeries, dancing with young fellows, with their old hands hanging over their shoulders. They are all dancing in Lisdoonvarna. Nobody is left sitting down. People dance from midday to three or four in the morning during a whole week. It's completely crazy.

I am not yet dealing with people personally on a systematic basis. It is more that if Dad is not here I would have words with the person myself if somebody phones. If I have never met or talked to the person before, I basically ask them about themselves, I tell them what we do and how we do it, and I get their address and I send them an application form. The application form is just the basic kind – their name, a photo, occupation, hobbies – just so you have it on paper in front of you.

We never did charge until a few years ago but now we take a charge of fifteen pounds just to cover ourselves. It is only fair, there is a lot of stamps and phone-calls going into it, not to mention all the time. It can be quite time-consuming to write all the letters.

After a while, when you have got back the application form, you get in touch with the person again and you get to know him or her a bit more. You can't ask them too many questions to start with because then you might put them off. The whole thing is like building up a relationship. They trust your opinion after a while when they get to like you, so the day you do turn around and say, 'There is a genuinely nice woman that I would like you to meet,' then they know that she is genuine. A lot of them wouldn't have the same trust in me as they have in Dad, as yet, but many would still value my opinion. There has been cases where men have not wanted to talk to me or they mightn't have felt comfortable talking to me, but there are other cases then where they feel like they are getting a woman's point of view as well which they feel can help them, and they appreciate that I am a woman.

If people are not on the phone you write to them. A lot of them actually prefer that you write because they might have to use a neighbour's phone or there might be other family around and they can be very shy about it. Especially if Willie Daly's name comes up, then people will know straight away that you are dealing with a matchmaker and they can get a bit funny about it and start to tease the person or whatever. Eventually, when it is time for it, maybe you write to a man to tell him about a particular lady, that 'She is such and such, she is nice, will you be interested?' You would give all the details, what age she is, what occupation she has and so on, everything you know and, 'You seem to be what she is looking for, do you want to meet her?' And you do the same to her. He is into this, into that, or if he has got kids you tell that, you have to let them know it all and keep no surprises.

It can get very difficult at times if you don't keep your head clear. The matchmaker has to know his people. You have to know where they are coming from, where they have been and where they are going; you have got to know their circumstances, a bit about their families, their area, even their neighbours; and you have to have it all in your head. You can't turn around when you talk to somebody and say, 'Wait, I will have to have a look in the book to see who you are.'

And you definitely need to talk personally to the people you are dealing with and preferably if possible even to meet them. If someone wrote you a letter and said 'I am such and such, this is me,' they could write anything. People are cute and shrewd, a bit like foxes. Most of the time they are sincere enough, but there has been a few odd cases where men have sent photos that were photos of them twenty years previous. Dad had a case when he brought down a woman to be introduced to a fellow that he hadn't met personally and obviously not checked up on well enough. They were looking for a man with black hair but all they could see was a man with grey hair. The one was a bit disappointed but she saw the fun of it all and she didn't mind. So you really need to know the people you are dealing with. Otherwise the man you are thinking about introducing a woman to might be a type of person that you wouldn't wish any woman in the world to be matched to.

If the two persons say yes to what you have suggested, you try to come up with a neutral ground where they can be introduced. She mightn't want it to be in her town and he mightn't want it to be in his town, and it might be too far for us to travel if it is half the way up the country.

Then you meet and you introduce them. I have been with Dad a few times when it happens. It is always in a public place. Our job is to make it all seem very natural so they don't feel like they are standing out in the cold. You make it so it is a nice little party of four or five or whatever. If they want to bring a friend along they can of course do that. Dad is great in those situations. He is so relaxed with people and he has got a great sense of humour. He never says anything negative that brings a conversation or a situation down.

You know what the people are into, so gradually you get the conversation going, and you might drop in something that the man is doing or interested in to get him talking or something that she is into to get her talking, and once they start talking, after fifteen, twenty minutes you know yourself if it is going grand and if it is you may leave and travel back with the mission more or less completed, and if not they might need a little bit more encouragement.

Some men are too shy the first time to ask for the woman's phone-number, but then they would get back to us and ask if we could help them to meet again, and you would know after having seen them together if, for example, the woman liked the man or not. If you feel and know – she might have told you – that she didn't like him, you wouldn't give him any false hope about it. But you have to really know if it hit or not between them because if there is the slightest chance that they could still meet you have to take it. If not, you say it just didn't work out for her or for him or whichever one it is. It can be a bit tricky. You feel sorry for them because they are both very awkward about it, especially if one person likes the other person a lot more. But then they are on the phone a few weeks later asking, 'Well, have you anybody else for me?'

Matchmaking can appear to outsiders to be a kind of last resort, which it isn't at all. Some people that contact us just ask if we believe that there is another way they can go about meeting somebody without having to go through the matchmaker. They don't want you to do it for them, they just want you to give bits of advice.

Others may have been in relationships before, relationships that split up for one reason or another and they never got back with anybody for maybe seven, eight years, something which happens an awful lot. After those years they might have forgotten how to meet somebody or got a bit shy, or maybe they have not been socialising and they want to get out of that circle that they are in, and they might come to us to be introduced to somebody. A lot of the time you can give them such courage and confidence in themselves by talking to them that they end up going out meeting people on their own.

As often as possible we try and encourage people to go out and socialise even while we are in the process of finding someone to introduce them to. We tell them that they have to travel, that they are not going to meet anyone in their home town unless they are introduced to somebody that is brought in there. When I say travel it might only be twenty miles down the road, to Ennis or Lisdoonvarna or to other different towns around here. That would for us in this area be regarded as travelling to foreign places.

People are not in a rush. They don't come up to you and say that they want to meet a woman in three weeks time. A few people might already be thinking what the next one could be like when they are meeting the first one, but with them you simply have to put your foot down.

What I prefer are the romantic trail-rides. I like them because I am with the same people for a whole week and it is so much easier to get to know them then. It gives me time enough to come to a conclusion about the person, to see whether he is genuine about what he is putting across to you or not.

We arrange these romantic trail-rides between April and October when it is warm enough to ride horses comfortably. It's usually six days on the Carrick Mountains up the back here, and around the Burren. It is so beautiful, so romantic, it is a brilliant setting, it is something like out of a movie when we ride off into the sunset. We have one evening when we ride down onto the beach and we have a barbecue before we ride back in the dark. It's hard to imagine if you haven't been out there, but it is very romantic. I love the atmosphere myself and it certainly does help to get people into the right frame of mind to meet somebody.

In certain cases we would advertise it as a week for people who are looking for a husband or a wife or a partner and in other cases we just advertise it as a romantic trail-ride. Sometimes we even get couples that are already married but who will come maybe to revitalise their marriage again, but normally it is single people coming looking for a partner. A lot of them can't even ride but they enjoy it just as well. It can actually be very good when somebody doesn't know how to do it. Say, you have got a person who can ride and a person who can't, then the one that can will help the other along. Horses seem to bring out the tender side of people, especially in men. They just seem a lot softer around horses.

We often ride up to six, seven hours a day but for people that can't ride we try to take it nice and easy. The person that has had too much of riding can of course get off and whoever can ride then can have a good gallop for themselves. I hate it myself if I am out on the track for my own enjoyment and if someone that can't ride is holding the whole thing back.

They come from everywhere to do the trail-rides. There is a lot of Americans and people from the Continent, but also a lot of Irish people. They would be mostly in their thirties to their fifties. I suppose it gets harder as you get older to get up on the back of a horse.

We sleep in bed-and-breakfasts and sometimes we travel to something like Ballynalackan Castle for a night ride up there, and then we might go on until Ballyvaughan to stay in a hostel there or maybe to camp out. It all depends on what the people are into. Some of them love the nightlife so much in Ennistymon and other places around here that they prefer to stay in the one place to get to know the locals. It's not just people that are out on horses that meet each other, they meet other

103

people outside of the group too. Sometimes we even might have someone down in Cork that has been on our books for a while and we put him or her up for the weekend to be able to introduce them as well.

Everyone is usually very nicely tired after the trek and whenever they have had enough in the evening we park the horses and we bring them out and they get a good feed before we take them around to different pubs. It is not about drinking – a lot of people don't even drink – it is the pub atmosphere and the dancing that counts. Dancing has a lot to do with it. When you dance you have got the movement, you are not restricted and you are face to face with each other. It is not like being at a disco where you can't talk or even see each other. Waltzing is a big thing with middle-aged people. You usually get three sets of waltzes in a row, so if the woman likes a man enough she will stay with him for the three waltzes and if not she makes an excuse after the first dance is up.

There's a funny story about something that happened during these trail-rides a few years ago. I think there is something very Irish about what happened, or at least I can't imagine it happening anywhere else in the time we're living in, not in the western world anyway.

Often when you are out riding and you pass a house of old people, they grab you and take you off your horse and bring you in for a cup of tea and a chat. It still happens today. But there was this particular woman up in the mountains whose house you had to pass. The only other way was to jump a few walls, but half the time you couldn't because the people on the ride weren't able to ride fast enough for it, they weren't able to jump. This woman would literally come out and hold your horse by the bit until you got off, and she would bring the women she took a fancy to into the kitchen, leaving the men outside holding the horses. If she had a woman in the kitchen whom she discovered that she didn't like or maybe she thought she was too cocky or whatever, then she would send her out. It was a good laugh and nobody was hurt by it. It was a lovely old thatched cottage, a bit black inside from the soot of the turf but very nice, and we had our cups of tea and biscuits or whatever it would be, and then after a while, when you were sitting down, the woman would parade her six sons one by one through the kitchen. They were big strapping fellows – they wouldn't be my cup of tea, now – but of course the American women got a great kick out of it. Believe it or not but this woman ended up matching three or four of her sons that way.

They have all left now. The eldest son went off to America with a woman a couple of years ago and the mother soon packed up and followed on and that's the last I have heard of her. She was really a bit of a handful.

A lot of the time the women head back to America with their Irishman. That is a dream come true for a lot of people around here. There is still a lot of Irish people that would love to be in America; it's like America is the place where anything you wish or want can happen. And I suppose women find it lonely around here, and you can understand that as well. They mightn't have a next-door neighbour for three, four miles. There is a lot of holiday houses here at the moment and it might look like a place that is well populated, but you have to remember that a lot of these houses are empty all winter and it can be very quiet and cold then. Have no illusions about that.

Pat Tierney

MY INTEREST IN poetry began when I was in a school for slow learners and handicapped children when I was about thirteen years of age. I remember writing my first poem there, and how the teacher said to me, 'Did you really write that?' But nobody followed it up, nobody ever tried to guide or drag me into what I was obviously interested in.

When I was sixteen years of age I was locked up. I had been stealing from cars. At that time I was living on the street. I had no home. I was an orphan. One day I came across a book of poems by the American poet Eugene Field. There was one poem there called 'Little Boy Blue' that I have never forgotten. It was the first poem that I learned off. The poem was written about the poet's nephew who had died in his sleep, a little boy, I think four years old. I thought there was so much sensitivity in the poem. It was certainly a sensitivity that I had never experienced in my childhood, or in my upbringing, in all the institutions that I had been in. Somehow that poem put me in touch with my own sensitivities and with my own emotions. It was at that point that I became seriously interested in poetry. I think there is a natural beauty in everything that is around us, if only we can see it and sense it and recognise it. I recognise it, I see it and I sense it in poetry.

During the following years, I had a lot of experience travelling around and going around trying to find my mother and all this kind of business. Eventually I ended up in America, where I spent eight years, one of them in Newfoundland on the eastern seaboard of Canada. I got to Newfoundland one Sunday morning and discovered that this was a province where I wouldn't find any kind of formal work. But I found a pub along a lonely isolated road where there was going to be a dance that same afternoon. I got permission from the owner to play my mouth-organ outside as people were coming in. I made perhaps twelve, thirteen dollars on it.

It was an atrociously wet day, so I went inside after the crowd and sat in a corner. The band had started playing, and I wrote a little poem for them. It was a rhyme rather than a poem; I wouldn't elevate it to that status. During the break I gave it to one of the band members, not expecting him to read it out, but he did, and I received an enthusiastic round of applause for it, plus drinks that started coming up from right, left and centre. I got talking to some of the locals, and they invited me to stay in their homes. I wrote a few more ballads and poems about the local area and decided that that would be my trade for the duration of my time in Newfoundland. So I started travelling from village to village writing ballads. I usually wrote about the history of the village and the local characters. I developed a method for it. At the end of day one in a village, I would have gotten the names of all the local landmarks, and then I would find someone who was interested in local history. On the second day, I would write the ballad; there might be as many as a hundred lines in it. On the third and fourth day, I would sell it for whatever people wanted to offer. And if there was a festival in some larger town, I would write a ballad especially for it and present it to the organisers.

After nine months of travelling, I eventually came to St John's, where I got into trouble with immigration authorities, but I managed to give them the slip and came back across the border into America again. In America I did a lot of therapy, and by the time I was heading back to Ireland, I felt like I kind of could 'leave my past behind me'. I was hungry for life in a way that I had never been before.

That was 1988. Since then I have been reciting poems on the streets of Dublin, and indeed in festivals and *fleadh cheoil* around Ireland. What I do is, I stand on the street, I put down my chamber-pot, the poet's pot as I call it, and a sign which has maybe thirty or forty titles of poems on it so people can have their pick. I usually keep around a hundred poems in my head. The shortest, for the moment, is a poem of one line by Susan Gatley about middle-aged crisis. At the other extreme you'll find a long poem, such as 'The Stolen Child' by William Butler Yeats, or one of my own poems, like 'Invaders' Perspective,' a poem about the political situation in the North. I am constantly reading poetry to see if there is anything I can use for the street. It's not all poems that are suitable for that kind of reading.

Reciting poetry is not the same as any other kind of busking. You don't just stand up and get going like you would if you played an instrument. It doesn't work like that. I have often felt like a lunatic standing on the street reciting poetry, trying to attract an audience, and the way people look at me they obviously think I am a lunatic as well. Poetry busking is different. It requires a tremendous amount of personality to actually make it work. The way you do it is, you put down your gear and start teasing people going up and down the street. You say things like: 'How are you doing, do you want to hear a good one?' Meaning a good poem. Or, 'Anyone there for poetry, the best of poetry here, recommended by the archbishop. You wouldn't see the likes of it in a Baghdad bazaar.' Or anything like that. People smile when you throw these things at them. What you really are involved in is a trawling exercise. You are trawling, trawling and trawling, and eventually you do get someone that stops and listens, and once you have got one person and have started to recite for her or him a crowd will build up. Sometimes there can be a hundred people listening, and some of them could be standing there for a full half hour. Others mightn't like the particular poem that you are reciting, or they are out shopping or whatever they are doing, and move on after only a few lines, but at least they acknowledge that you are there by stopping.

People often say to me, 'Oh, you are reciting poetry on Grafton Street, you must do well out of the Yanks,' or the Germans or the Dutch. That is not true. It is the Irish people that support my reciting of poetry. Very few Irish people would throw five pence into the pot. Most of them would throw fifty pence or a pound. I think Irish people have more understanding of what I am doing. I believe one reason for that is that we are only three or four generations away from when this type of reciting was pretty common in our country. Michael Moran, known as Zozimus, was the last one who did it in Dublin. I am not sure, but I think he died in the twenties. [He died in 1846] So, I have only revived this tradition. Today we are a couple of guys doing it. I think Irish people somehow are aware through their history that this is a part of our heritage and our culture, and that's why they support it, and why they took to it so quickly when I started doing it. It was just a matter of presenting it again to them.

I have never had anything but compliments for what I am doing. And many poets are quite proud to see their names displayed on the street. In fact, a couple of well-known poets have come to me and asked why I am not reciting one of their poems. The answer to that would be, first of all, I only recite what I like, which is not at all the analytical type of poetry that is more written for the university auditorium than for the ordinary man in the street. The top ten of what is today regarded as our finest living poets in Ireland are all in the universities. I honestly don't like a lot of the poetry that is published today, but other people do, and that's fine for me, we have to have our differences.

I haven't written poetry now in a long time. I wrote a couple of collections, but then I moved away from it. There are always other things that occupy me, and to make a really good poet out of me would take too much time and disciplined work, and I have none of that. In fact, I don't really like writing. I can only do it if I have everything ready in my head so I can finish the job quickly. My book, the one I wrote in prose, *The Moon On My Back*, is about 110,000 words. I wrote three drafts of it longhand in twelve weeks. Some days I was writing seventeen or eighteen hours. The writing was a challenge, but an even bigger challenge was actually to think about what was going to happen once the book was published. You know, I was the first one in Ireland that went public in writing about being HIV positive.

At the time I was involved in work with a youth club and I was also teaching children how to write poetry. That was a voluntary thing; it is something I enjoy doing. So when I had the book finished and it was brought to the printer, I got a letter typed up and dropped a copy of it to all the parents. It said something like: 'You know that I have spent some years in America, but what you don't know is that I got involved in intravenous drug use for some time, and that I now find that I am HIV-positive. If you have any questions or queries about it, please telephone me or drop up and see me any time.' And I recommended them to tell their children about it, and that they too, if they had anything they would like to ask or something that they were curious about, that they too could come to me and I would answer them the best I could.

What followed showed that the stigma was more in my head than in the heads of other people. No one threw stones at me. The opposite of what I had feared happened: a lot of people showed that they cared about me, and many congratulated me for my courage to go public with it. Today people trust me, and many people for one or another reason want to talk to me about it. People here in Ballymun are in general great, which is, I'm sure, difficult to believe if one only follows what is said about Ballymun and its people in the media.

There was a series filmed down here a few years ago called *The Family*, written by Roddy Doyle. I formed a committee – Positive Images Ballymun – to fight the sort of image which was being associated with Ballymun in that series. They brought in bags of rubbish, they sprayed graffiti on the walls, they made sure in the filming that the estate was very clearly identified. The thing is that a series like *The Family*, which was about abuse in the home, should have been filmed in an ordinary housing estate of the type you'll find anywhere in Ireland, and not in an area that is so obviously Ballymun. There is only one Ballymun in Ireland, and everybody knows it by its high towers. A series like that that is filmed in Ballymun only serves to give the public the false perception that everyone that lives in Ballymun is a scumbag, that there is graffiti all over the place, that people throw rubbish everywhere, and that they are the type of people that you would rather not be around. I fought very strongly against that. The type of people you find in Ballymun are the same type of people that you find living anywhere. You find people who are doing drugs, who are selling drugs; you find nurses who work in hospitals, people who work for the Dublin Corporation; you find people who own shops in and around the city; you have people here from Nairobi, from all over the world, people in flats, in houses, people with families, grandchildren, dogs, flowers in the garden; but the media choose never to focus on the positive sides.

Ballymun is more socially and politically vibrant than most other housing estate areas in the country. There are an incredible amount of things going on here. A quick look in the Ballymun directory and everybody will understand what I am talking about. We have every sort of club conceivable, and there are a couple of Irish schools in the area, and we have a women's refuge, and we are proud of it. A middle-class or an upper-class area wouldn't even allow a women's refuge, as it might lower the value of their property, and it would also give the impression that everything is not so rosy in their rose gardens. They wouldn't want a travellers' halting site either. We have one a mile up the road, and there is never any problem with that. But all these positive things that I am lining up don't mean that there aren't problems in the area. We have lots of them.

This area has one fundamental problem. It was built twenty-seven years ago as a short-term measure to deal with the housing crisis in the city. The idea was to put the blocks up, use them for ten years and then pull them down again. So there was no proper structure built in, no proper centres for the local communities. They were not building an estate which was going to be a solid community; they were building a kind of refugee camp that people were supposed to come to only for a little while before they found their own houses. It became a transient area. Many of the people here mightn't have had so much respect for their environment, because it was just something they were passing through, rather than saying, 'This is where we are going to raise our children. This is where our grandchildren are going to live.' I think this is a psychological element which has affected the way in which the area has turned out.

But then you also have the absolutely criminal neglect of the estate by Dublin Corporation. Just take a simple thing like the lifts. I can set my clock by how the lift in the tower in which I live breaks down, and I live on the fourteenth floor, so don't tell me it isn't a problem, and I still have people living above me. Dublin Corporation says it is because of the vandalism that is going on. In the part of the estate that they have refurbished, they put in cameras in the lifts, because now they were going to catch the vandals. As it turns out, the lifts over there are breaking down as frequently as they are here, and no vandals are ever caught. It's a mechanical problem. There's no quality in the material, it's junk. Take another example of neglect: only 10 per cent of the kids out here – and there are many kids here, Ballymun has a very young population – have any organised playground. Look out from my balcony and you'll see no swings around, no nothing for the kids. Another example: there are about 22,000 people living in Ballymun, and you can't find a simple thing like a pair of socks in the shopping centre. It is really disheartening to see how the people are treated here. If I had the health and money, I would run as an independent candidate outside the party system for the people of Ballymun in the next election. I think I am a capable campaigner. I have been fighting on issues since I was seventeen years old.

For some time I have been involved in the Magdalen Memorial Committee. We created it to raise the issues that were associated with the history of these women and what happened to their children. The Magdalen women, as they are called, were Irish women who were sent into those different laundry institutions for one reason or another. Some of them were sent there by the state, but more often by a local priest. Say, for example, a girl was staying out late in the evenings, and the father went to the priest and talked to him about it. The priest would say that he could get her a job in Dublin where she would be looked after, and the girl would be brought to one of these laundries run by the nuns in the convent, convents founded to rescue 'fallen women', and basically would be made to work there for the rest of their lives without getting any money for it. Their names were changed when they got there, their identities were taken from them. They were now known as Magdalen women and referred to by the nuns as 'penitents'. In the Bible, Mary Magdalen was the prostitute that bathed and dried Jesus's feet, and all these women were branded as prostitutes even if they were not. They were given names like Magdalen Mary, Magdalen Veronica, and all these kind of stupid Christian Catholic names of saints. There are still a couple of these women around, but they are old now. It's not because the nuns have reached some kind of enlightment or something like that that this kind of slavery is over. It's because they wouldn't get away with that kind of shit any more. The state and the people wouldn't allow it.

About two years ago the nuns in the convent on Sean MacDermott Street in Dublin decided they wanted to sell some land, because they had lost money on the stock exchange, on GPA shares, and needed cash. There were two graveyards on the property. One for the Magdalen women and one for the nuns. The ground where the Magdalen women were buried was deconsecrated, diggers were brought in and the whole graveyard was dug up. The bones that were found were taken on the back of a pick-up to Glasnevin cemetery where they were cremated and put in 133 urns, and stacked on top of each other in two graves which were filled up, and that was it, thought the nuns, but not so. A woman and myself decided that we were going to try to get a public memorial service for these Magdalen women. We collected 10,000 signatures outside the GPO in six days calling for a memorial service, and a week later it was held. Since then we have been trying to get some kind of recognition of these women's existence. The situation now is that we are going to unveil a plaque to their memory in Stephen's Green in the middle of Dublin. I have been working on the wording for the plaque, and the president, Mary Robinson, is coming to unveil it for us. That, for me, would be the conclusion of a very worthwhile campaign. Hopefully the memory of these women and their history won't be forgotten so easily. At least when people read the plaque, if they want to go on then and do research about the women, they can do it.

One of the reasons that I got involved in the Magdalen women is, I believe, that I myself was put in an institution when I was born, and my mother was taken away to another institution in Tuam for a little while before she started to work in Galway as a domestic servant in a school run by the Church. She would have washed clothes and scrubbed floors and all that. And many of the boys that I would have been raised with in the institutions would have their mothers in places like the Magdalen institutions. Because I myself had been in institutions, I understood what these women had gone through in their lives. And it was such a degrading thing for these women, not only to let them slave for nothing all their lives, but then to dig them up from their graves so the nuns could make some money. The most obnoxious element of the whole scenario was that the remains were cremated. Cremation while these women were alive was a sin in the eyes of the Catholic Church. It is only recently that the Catholic Church has come around to cremation. Those women would have been absolutely horrified if they could ever know that their remains would be dug up and thrown into a fire and burnt.

I don't know from where I get the energy to keep fighting. I think I am actually very angry. I think I am angry about the way my own life has turned out, although I have to say that, compared to many people's lives, I have had a great life and a great spirit and energy. But here I am, thirty-eight years of age, and I would say that if I am alive in two years time that will be about as much as I will get out of it, because my immune system is very badly damaged.

There is a sense that somehow all those injustices and the oppression I was a victim of during my childhood and while I was growing up, that they have all contributed greatly to the fact that I have AIDS today. It is all interconnected. One reason that I wrote *The Moon On My Back* was that I wanted to contextualise what had happened to me, and why it had happened. I didn't want people to say, 'There is Pat Tierney who has AIDS because he was involved in intravenous drug use.' I wanted to put the whole thing into context and tell about the incidents and the situations and the circumstances which somehow over a period of years brought this man to the point where he was taking drugs and alcohol. What was it in his life that was so horrific that he subconsciously wanted to blur all of these memories? I think I have AIDS today because of the way I was raised by the institutions and their people, because of the way I was beaten, sexually molested, psychologically abused, the whole mess which was my life. I frankly think that somebody out there owes me something, but I don't expect to ever get anything. Anyway, this is possibly one of the reasons why I am such a fighter. I don't want anybody to get away with any kind of injustice.

Some time ago, it must have been the evening when Dublin won the All-Ireland Final, I was walking over O'Connell Bridge. I saw a child with a Dublin flag in one hand and a box in the other, begging. It was late, it was about eight o'clock. Then I saw how a big hefty fellow in a wheelchair rolled over to the boy and started beating him, before he took the flag and the box with the money. Fuck this, I said to myself, and went over to the guy in the wheelchair. I whipped the flag out of his hand, took the box with the money from him and told him that if I ever caught him doing a thing like that again I would throw him and his wheelchair into the river. I just can't see things like that and not react. Most people say, it's none of your business, but I'm sorry, it is. We are all in the humanity business, and some of us have to take risks and stick our necks out. Otherwise injustice, by institution or individual, will go unchecked, and that's just not good enough.

Eunice McCarthy

I THINK THAT EACH race has deeply rooted images stored among its memories, formed and preserved over long periods of time, lying dormant, forgotten, but not altogether lost. Many of the beliefs and customs of our ancient Celtic culture persist in Irish attitudes even today, in various forms and shapes. They survive in curious and often surprising ways.

Celtic mythology demonstrates a deep understanding of both nature and the human psyche, in the way the key actors – gods, goddesses, heroes, heroines and mortals – relate to one another. In today's world, a post-modern society or information age, I sense that we are now experiencing a new and subtle awareness of a need to take a penetrating look at our cultural traditions, including mythologies, to examine their strengths and their continued relevance to us.

We in Ireland are at a crossroads. Many of our distinctive rituals have disappeared. Some of these may reflect the depression, deprivation and exclusion experienced by the Irish over the past few hundred years and, as such, people are content with their disappearance – it marks progress into a more 'humane' society. Others may not have found a transformative 'face' in modern development.

Looking back into our psychic past, there are certain core themes that can be distilled from our Celtic culture, and which we could revise and reconstruct within our present modern-day world context. I think these themes can be drawn on to inform

119

our construction of present-day realities.

One theme which has a strong resonance for me is the sanctity of the land and the power of place. In the Celtic tradition land was sacred, and certain key locations on the land, such as Tara, had power. In mythology there is the *grá*, or love or fusion with the land. The Irish Celts had a whole vision for the sanctity of life and land, unified and harmonised together. The Goddess of Sovereignty, who mediates and represents the energies of the land, is well known in Irish mythological traditions. The Céide Fields site in County Mayo, recently excavated by Seamus Caulfield, demonstrates the deep ties between the people and their land going back some 5,000 years. The land and the environment was seen as a reality indivisible from human reality, and not viewed as dead matter. The entire landscape and environment was alive. The innate goodness of nature was a dominant theme: early Irish poetry talks all the time about rivers and streams, trees and animals, all in an alive way.

Today the ecological perspective has rediscovered the inter-connectedness and interdependence of the human person and ecological forces underlying what some call the spiritual dimension of life. The ecological perspective within the industrial and post-industrial framework alerts us to the way we have disassociated ourselves from our cultural context. Deep Celtic values are mirrored in the modern ecological concern for protection of the land, the sea and the atmosphere.

Another theme emergent from our Celtic culture is our oral tradition, which has been very creative, imaginative and powerful. It is reflected in our story-telling and legends. The complexity of our language has been refined to a high level of skill and artistry. Our Gaelic language carries within it both explicit and implicit messages relating to our values and what was significant and important to our ancestors over the millennia. A whole complex of story-telling revolved around the encounter of Saint Patrick and Oisín on his return from *Tír na nÓg*, the Otherworld, when all the other Fianna were long gone. These stories represented a meeting of the old Irish world, recounted in tales, stories and myths, and the new world of Christianity. They sensitively mapped out the strengths of the old, while at the same time taking on the challenge of the new. These dialogues could be viewed as a prototype for any major change process – a paradigm shift from one set of world views to another and a blending and integration of both views and approaches.

Originally Celtic lore and mythology were preserved orally. This was a culture in which the written word was either unknown or regarded as a trivialising influence. It contrasts sharply with the way, nowadays, information is stored in computers. We know that the Druids preserved immense stores of learning through memory alone. A well-defined art of memory was known in the older world, where it seems to have been closely allied to a visual, imaginative system of storing information.

The strength of our oral tradition is evident in our conversations, our dialogue, our discourse. Present-day expression of this oral tradition is that people like to converse, to narrate, to talk, to tell stories. New social gatherings, for example in pubs, which have replaced the firesides of old, are now also centres of story-telling. Work-places carry their own stories and tales, which overlap with other community tales. Time, space and place are needed for conversing, chatting and telling stories. 'Myth Information System' might be a more fruitful way of renaming and thinking about the communication and learning which goes on in work-places than 'Management Information Systems', which tend to be linear and mechanistic and lack human connectivity.

Imagination and complexity are expressed through our story-telling and our poetry and literature. Our poetic tradition was highly developed and the power of the tongue was deeply respected. Poets enjoyed a high social position in Ireland down to the seventeenth century, being more or less on a par with the chieftains and the bishop. The poet's disapproval, and his satire or *aor*, were very much feared, a bit like the media and TV of our time. Folklore often represented people as envying poets and wishing to emulate them. Poets were perceived as cultural heroes and heroines.

Involved in our mythology and mind is also this idea about the voyage, the journey. The sea that surrounded us had a force and mystery which lured us out. The voyage was the discovery. Thus the adventure, the voyage that incorporates uncertainty, risk, potential of great rewards and success, is a central theme of our story-telling. Saint Brendan's voyage to America in the year 536 is inspired by and is a relatively modern version of older mythological voyages. The journey to the Otherworld, to the supernatural, to the unconscious, was commonplace in Celtic mythology. Fionn MacCumhail and his warriors frequently entered the Otherworld, both as a world of peace and strangeness and a world of the fantastic – yet they always returned, maintaining their integrity.

The psycho-dynamics of these Celtic tales have not been probed. Modern psychoanalysts, like Jung, examined in great depth mythologies and cultures around the world, but he never looked at the Celtic mythology that envelops and surrounds us. Thus the wisdom that we have, or had, lies submerged, and full of possibilities for new understandings and insights. For example, the imagery of the Fianna riding out and then becoming transformed is both subtle and powerful. They appeared to be very comfortable exploring the Otherworld: they were grounded in this world and yet they could move in the next, unscathed in the sense that they didn't flounder. One suggestion for this strength is pointed out by the Celtic scholar Tomás Ó Cathasaigh, who explains that the Irish word *sidhe* means not only the Otherworld, but that it also means peace.

I think that we have lost that kind of understanding or ability to communicate with the unconscious. Nowadays people need to take drugs or psychedelic substances to enter the Otherworld, and when they do get locked in they might never return to a former state of reality integration.

The telling of culture tales, narratives, stories, legends, about heroes and heroines who were painted as having some quite exceptional powers, never failed to gain an audience. No doubt many of the listeners secretly longed to have similar abilities and power. In psychological terms they identified with the personage in the tales. For example, McClelland in his cross-cultural study of schoolchildren pointed out that where societies carry achievement stories in their everyday lore and in the educational system, children acquire achievement goals and set challenges for themselves. In other words, our store of stories, myths and legends can act as catalysts for innovative, challenging, risk-taking adventures and innovations, where the story content embodies the images, the road maps, the beliefs and the values that underpin creative and challenging enterprise and achievement.

These legends, rather than being viewed as 'tales of the fantastic' which people recount in the dark and dreary times to maintain an integrative psychic balance, may also be searched for hidden messages, the meaning and meta-knowledge locked into every word and sentence. The pattern of the story and the implicit views of the world, of nature and of the mind that are embedded in the tales encapsulate a rich reservoir of seeking awareness and understanding phenomena, whether spiritual, psychic or physical, from which we have separated ourselves over the millennia.

Irish psychologists celebrated the twenty-fifth anniversary of the Psychological Society of Ireland in 1994, and we published an issue of our journal entitled *The Irish Psyche*. I focused my contribution on 'work and mind' and called it 'Searching for Our Celtic Legacy.' I tried to distil and understand what there is in our indigenous Irish psychology that is seeping through from our Celtic tradition. Further – are there any resources and richnesses in our Celtic culture that we could embrace, and embody in our methods of working and collaborating into the second millennium?

Modern-day management theories are leaning more towards a non-linear, complex mode of conceptualisation of organisational systems which embodies uncertainty and chaos, rather than simple linear models of organisation. Now the cry is for managers who can innovate and who can handle diversity; for employees that are self-managing and self-leaders; a new awareness that we need more creativity instead of the old way of bashing it out of people. I believe that the Irish have a resource here, that we have an underlying current of creativity that could and should be tapped into.

A cross-cultural study conducted by Hofstede, a Dutch scholar, in forty countries, including Ireland, attempted to identify our cultural differences and similarities. One of the core dimensions distilled was 'avoiding uncertainty'. Countries that were high on 'uncertainty avoidance' included Japan, Austria and Germany, cultures that are characterised by structure and order. In comparison Ireland was relatively low on 'uncertainty avoidance'. The Irish managers indicated that they took uncertainty on board, that it was something they worked with: they did not feel threatened by uncertain and ambiguous situations.

It is not easy to explain why that is so, but we can maybe look at something that surrounds us – the coastline geography of our little island. Our coastline is very jagged and uneven. The thunderous Atlantic roars on our West Coast. I believe a natural phenomenon like that also enters the mind and forms it. There is nothing smooth in it; it's completely uneven and non-linear. In Holland you get this idea of lines. Everything is in lines. In Ireland both natural and mental phenomena present as more non-linear. Instead of going from A to B in a straight line, the psychic journey goes around in curves, then takes off in other directions. It is like Irish conversation, which is recursive and suddenly goes off in rambling tangents.

That non-linearity is, I think, one important factor in the Irish mind. I see it in how people relate to each other. People in Ireland on the whole don't say things or communicate in a very open or very straight manner. Frequently they don't say exactly what they want to say, they tend to go around and about and convolute the message. People from other countries often find the Irish very hard to understand. Americans, for example, are much more up-front. In Ireland, getting people to disclose their inner feelings is a slow process. Maybe it is about establishing trust with the other person and trying to find out who the other person is before disclosing anything of themselves, as if being circumspect. It is all very ambiguous. In one way I think it is a kind of protective device which a colonial people have developed to ward off undesirable situations and consequences. When Irish people come into stressful and tricky situations, they start laughing or telling jokes. There is a lot of anxiety underlying this language of repartee so peppered with jokes and laughs.

It is not only the mind that the Irish person covers up. It is also the body. For instance, people in general don't like to be seen naked in public showers. It was only recently with the rise of health centres that open showers were accepted. There is obviously a very strong repression of the body in Ireland. The Jansenistic form of Christianity that we imported in the last century very much spearheaded a spirit of the mind. Irish Catholicism became very abstract and moved away from the body, and people absorbed that split between body and mind that Descartes talks about on another level. In Ireland the split seems to have grown between sexuality and mind. This contrasts sharply with the situation in Celtic mythology where body and beauty were valued and respected and romanticised.

The paradox is that the Irish can present as authoritarian and conforming to religious rules and norms, while at the same time they are circumspect and non-disclosing. This non-linearity that we find in the Irish character suggests that we do not see things in a simple linear way, but that we see other complications in the situation as well. I think that comes through pretty clearly in Irish literature. The classic example is of course James Joyce, who epitomises the very non-linear mode, although within a certain structure. The Celtic stories show the same non-linearity: the hero goes off on a journey looking for something, but on the way he diverts on many other trips and adventures.

In an extreme psychological sense, chaos sounds like disorder, but we can also talk about it more in a sense of working with variety and creativity and difference. In the context of non-linearity, chaos really means complexity.

Modern civilisation is trying to order things more and more. I don't think we are allowing enough scope for the non-linear. When people say that the Catholic Church has authority, what they are really talking about is an order that is not, as it were, allowing scope for differences, for the non-linearity of the human being.

Non-linearity is something from our Celtic tradition that we could be losing, that we have to rediscover and to rethink how to value and hold. We can impose rigid order so that everything appears grand, but then the chaos which has been repressed erupts. Examples of underlying chaos includes recent revelations of child abuse in a context of order, where the family was inviolate and could not be examined despite cries for help relating to abuse and domestic violence. Where destructive chaos is repressed, the constructive element of chaos and complexity are submerged also, with traumatic consequences, in this instance, for those children and adults and institutions involved.

I would say one of the big problems of modern Ireland is non-communication about the darker side, in other words, destructive chaos or the non-linear. This is covered up and a facade of order is presented, without our facing the reflection and rethinking required to prevent and counter the destructive forces. These in turn can become resistant to change, but no learning reflexive mechanisms have been put in place.

It is generally accepted that a veil has been cast over the dynamics of family life. Resistance to opening the shell of silence which surrounds family life on our island has been poignantly revealed during the divorce debate since the mid-1980s, and has been further intensified in recent years with the

127

second divorce referendum which came before the people in the month of *Samhain*, the month of November 1995. In the ancient world, *Samhain* marked the change from one world to another, when we go from the summer and autumn into the nether world of the winter, into the unconscious or the soul space of our society.

Monica McGoldrick's work as a family therapist has drawn her into a journey seeking meanings of the Irish psyche and personality. She drew her insights from Irish-Americans in therapeutic settings. She describes the Irish as charming, jovial and 'cunnish', who bond together for a cause, especially a moral or a political cause, and yet they seem to suffer from a sense of isolation, sadness and tragedy.

These traits of withdrawal mirror those of the post-colonial personality which, as highlighted by the psychologist Vincent Kenny, exhibits a personal withdrawal which involves elaborations of the inner world, helplessness and passivity. Helplessness associated with a negative perception of the self can also be linked with a loss of self-confidence. A focus on the inner world is further associated with fantasy, magical thinking, superstition and creativity.

The way the Irish handle hostility and aggression also presents a paradox. Hostility in the family when not disguised, as with ridicule or sarcasm, is generally dealt with by a silent build-up of resentments, culminating in the cutting off of the vital relationship without a word. The modern playwright Brian Friel has frequently, for example in *Philadelphia, Here I Come* or *Dancing at Lughnasa*, captured the severance of contact and of communication so characteristic of the traditional Irish family. The stereotype of the wild Irish temper contrasts with the tendency not to express anger within the family.

Irish friendliness can parallel a tendency towards distancing at family level. Further, the Irish sense of humour, which can be identified as one of the great strengths of the Irish, can also embody a mystifying and double-bind character, involving a form of banter which says one thing and means the other. Teasing and ridicule are especially common in Irish family relationships, while closeness is avoided.

While the colonial personality is characterised by helplessness, dependency, ambivalence, lack of self-confidence, it is of interest today to see the rise and evolution of communal empowerment. This empowerment is driven by marginal groups which have been invisible for a long time. These include in particular the womens' movement, the peace movement and the ecology movement, which represent in turn groups who were or are marginalised and have edged their way more and more towards centre stage. In the process they are empowering communities and small groups to communicate, to speak out, to influence the central decision-making on issues that impact on them. They are moving from a state of dependency, of learned helplessness, the colonial model, to empowerment and power sharing.

Communal sharing and caring comes through as a central value in Celtic culture. In the twelfth-century *Ban Seanachais* text, which recounts the lore of women, the tribal co-operative system is documented, as is the care devoted to diverse members of the group. The handicapped child in Irish is called *duine le Dia*, a person of God, much more kindly than the derogatory legal terminology which was in vogue up to recent years.

In the old Irish communal arena, men and women were identified as individuals, with their own idiosyncratic personalities, and as part of a group, with a place in their living location. Our Celtic tradition suggests a cultural conception of the individual that links him or her to the family, the social group, the cultural and natural background, and not merely offering a definition of the individual as someone separate and distinct from other people.

In psychology we talk about those people who relate to things, and those who relate to people. The Irish, I believe, tend to relate to people. Thinking back to a study I carried out in Shannon in which I was looking at how workers experienced the industrialisation process, it was almost as if the attraction of their co-workers brought them to Shannon rather than the jobs that were on offer. It is of interest that many people I talked with didn't see the job as the type of work that they really wanted to do. They were all much more idealistic, in the sense that they wanted to be nurses, doctors, teachers. The jobs that were highly valued were jobs that related to people. For them, being on the factory floor did not truly reflect their identity, as might be the case among workers in the north of England. They saw the job in the factory as a jumping off ground to more attractive work abroad. Mainly they stated they would emigrate and travel to get the job they wanted.

Even those masses of Irish who emigrated to the USA since the 1850s, whether they advanced through the trade unions, or the police force or the political party, they were drawn to 'people work' – they affiliated and grouped together and worked with people in service areas. And in this society at home, today, people group together in the pub. One could say that the pub phenomenon is not about drinking, it's about meeting and socialising. And not long ago it was common that people congregated in country houses, in people's homes, where they danced and were comfortable together.

Looking back through our traditions, and learning how to navigate in the world of societal culture, draws us to the meaning of our experience at the end of the twentieth century. We have turned away from much of our inherited wisdoms, from our language and our rituals. However, while we have lost a lot of the language we are reviving the music and we are retrieving Irish dance. Irish dance was rejected in favour of international dances until a few years ago. Then, suddenly, there was a new confidence, a confidence that this dance is good. 'Riverdance', as a metaphor, taps the concept of the journey, the movement, the synchronisation and the harmony that the Irish psyche encapsulates. Irish dancing is a very complex process with a great sense of rhythm in it. There is variety and variance and creativity in it, and it is not just going off into nowhere. I think there is a wonderful aliveness in the mind that seeps through Irish music and dance. It embodies a tremendous speed and power. It also links us to our feelings and intuitions which, as Jung has stated, are our most reliable guides into the Otherworld, the unconscious, the next millenium.

Margaret Mac Curtain

Yes, THERE IS much appreciation of, and even lip-service paid to the notion of Irish spirituality, and whether in fact we are a people who treasure spirituality. Contemporary questioning about the nature of Irish spirituality is sceptical about its reality. Twenty years ago it would have been accepted by many people, Protestants as well as Catholics, Methodists as well as Church of Ireland, Jewish people as well as agnostics, that there was in Irish culture a quality of metaphysics around death, around birth and around family, which had nothing in common with the glib category of 'family' values that you hear today, trotted out by people who want to preserve these values. There was a perception that Irish people, whether they believed in a Christian way of life, or whether they were post-Christian, or whether they were from a Judaic background, that they possessed a depth of awareness around the meaning of life that one didn't find, for example, in the bigger island next door, more specifically in England rather than Scotland. I think the legacy of an inherited spirituality still exists in parts of Scotland, in the highlands and the islands.

I am a very good example of that legacy myself, of that sense of a past. I remember when I was a student in university I came into the big room where the professors saw students and visitors. I was dressed in my Dominican habit with the veil and the long white robes. The professor was talking about the place of genealogy in Irish culture to a historian from Luxembourg, who worked in Switzerland, a very cosmopolitan man. When the professor saw me, he said, 'Let me introduce you to Margaret, my student. She is Celtic on both sides. Her name, Mac Curtain, comes from a very ancient family that goes back to the tenth century, and on her mother's side, McKenna, she comes from an equally old family that is associated with Monaghan.' I was surprised at what he said: I had never thought of that, that in Ireland names that are taken as family names or as married names actually go back hundreds of years, and that people carry an awareness of this archaic genealogy.

That brings me to the basis for assuming that there is a spirituality on the island, and the perception that the Irish are a spiritual people, which really is linked to the presence of Celtic civilisation in the island. The fact that the Roman march was halted at Durham and on the borders of Scotland meant that the Romans abandoned their invasion of Celtic realms. It was then a Celtic civilisation which received the beginnings of Christianity in Ireland.

We know that the Celtic people were a spiritual people. We know from their sculptures, which have been discovered in those parts of Europe where they came from, their love of nature from their belief that God, this creator of being, is present in every animal, every insect, in every creature on this planet.

The blending of Christianity and Celtic culture was a very fascinating one. It lasted a long time, from the fifth century to the Norman period some 600 years later. This is very tangible in the Irish countryside. People who suffered in the time of hunger during the periodic famines, or people who suffer a loss of a child, or an accident on a farm where cows are mutilated or die from some strange disease, still tend to go to holy wells, or to invoke the local saint, both invariably embedded in the Celtic past.

Recently I was down in a very beautiful part of West Cork that I hadn't visited for a few years, Gougane Barra, which is a place of pilgrimage around the hermitage of the founding saint of Cork city, Saint Finbar. Gougane Barra is set into a remote beautiful lake surrounded by hills. One is very alone there, but one is never lonely, because people are always moving around the small island praying and honouring this shadowy holy man of the sixth century who was a hermit. And then, close by, in Ballyvourney, a village in Gaelic-speaking West Cork, where you still hear a beautiful Irish spoken, there is a shrine to another Celtic saint, Saint Gobnait. Seamus Murphy, the noted sculptor, was commissioned by the local people to carve a statue of Saint Gobnait, and there she stands holding in her stone hands a large bee. Saint Gobnait is the patron saint of beekeepers, and on her feast day many beekeepers still honour her and pray to her for a fine harvest of honey.

These old memories are alive and certainly belong to the folk-life of rural Ireland, and the rural people then bring them into the cities with them. There is a tremendous interaction between city and country in Ireland. It is very easy from any of our cities to be out in the country in thirty minutes. Think of Dublin and parts of rural Wicklow, or rural Meath. Think of Cork and the whole hinterland of West Cork, and also think of Belfast and the wonderful County Down that invites you from Belfast to explore parts of the island that are closely associated with Saint Patrick. Again, interestingly, Saint Patrick comes from the same Celtic period. Saint Patrick, the founder of Christianity in Ireland, gave it a local, non-institutionalised character that seemed to take into itself an ecology or sense of a locality, an ecology of respect for nature, which was in tune with Celtic reverence for the earth and sun.

135

It is intriguing when one looks at the belief that there is a tradition of spirituality, not just in Celtic Christianity but in the whole recent past of Irish society, and that that spirituality was intrinsic not just to one's adoption of a particular creed, such as Roman Catholicism or Presbyterianism, but was, as I said, the foundation of the spiritual character of the society. We share this with Northern Ireland. It is something, I believe, which goes much deeper than the present Troubles of the twentieth century.

From my own studies, and I remain a historian of the reformation centuries, it seems to me that neither the coloniser – who was a Protestant 'settler', either Presbyterian or Church of England or later Church of Ireland – nor the native who chose the Tridentine, the Roman Catholic form of reformation at the end of the sixteenth century, that neither group discarded as unnecessary baggage the heritage of the Middle Ages.

Even when you live in a country with ruined mediaeval monasteries, which were unroofed during those reformation and colonising centuries, the centuries of conquest, and enter those old monasteries, you will find that many of the local farmers and people were buried within the precincts over a long period. There is a living link between the past and the living present, and the link, curiously enough, is the subject of death.

Death was close to the Celtic spirit. The Celts honoured death, they grieved over death, but they also felt that it was in some way an experience that need not be shunned. We do not have a wonderful piece of statuary like the 'Dying Gaul', the Celtic warrior that was found in France, but we have the legend of Cúchulainn, the young man who died for a cause. The legend runs right through the twentieth-century mythology of warfare. It is, so to speak, a metaphysical heroic death-wish, dangerous when taken to the lengths that it was taken in 1916 in the rebellion in Dublin. Dangerous also when it has been taken to the limits, such as in a movement like the IRA, which is among the most powerful and persistent clandestine movements of the twentieth century when you test it, but at the same time very beguiling to young people. Here is the wonderful mythical hero, Cúchulainn, the Hound of Ulster, pledged to guard the territory of Ulster from the men of the other parts of Ireland, who, finally, encounters his best friend, selected on another side, in single combat, and they fight to the death, with all the mythology of the black raven croaking on the tree above them, and a pervading sense of tragedy where young men die for their country. W. B. Yeats worried greatly that in his play *Cathleen Ní Houlihan* he glorified this kind of young death for a country. In his poem 'The Man and the Echo' he asks: 'Did that play of mine send out Certain men the English shot?'

We have this strange connection with death in Ireland. Sometimes I wonder if it is because we are totally surrounded by water! By and large we are a fishing people. Go to Donegal, to Burtonport, and you see there a monument to eleven young fishermen who were drowned in the 1970s. You get the same overtones in Synge's *Riders to the Sea*, when old Maura says: 'They are all dead now' – her three sons, drowned in the sea and brought back on a trestle with their *báinín* jumpers dripping with seawater, to be mourned by the local community – and she says: 'They are all gone now, and there is nothing more the sea can do to me.' That kind of fatalism is part of the Irish psyche, and I really quite honestly don't believe that any amount of information technology will remove from society that inbuilt inclination in the Irish towards thinking about the profound meaning of life, the notion of death and the honouring of death by funerals or, wherever it still lingers as a custom, the wake, this mixture of the comic and the sorrowful in the celebration of death around the corpse of a relative.

The intriguing question, of course, that now is asked is: will Ireland become just another pragmatic, commercially orientated country, successful in terms of a progressive and healthy economy? Will Ireland be able to achieve that, and at the same time retain this half wistful, totally attractive type of spirituality that you encounter for example in people with disabilities? There is an extraordinary fortitude in people who have suffered great losses, particularly through the death of children, or the death of a loved one. Will they be able to sustain that loss if they lose that connecting link to the past, if, as has been predicted, the Irish move from the devotional structure of a Church-based sacramental life into a kind of an 'un-sacramentalised' Christianity? I think this question engages us all. I mean, we are all trying to look into the crystal ball and say, well, how will young people in twenty years time, who have not had a faith-world buttressed by the routine of a Church that ministers very actively, retain this heritage which is such an old one?

We are standing on the threshold of something very important for Ireland, and that is a questioning of the role of the priest, or the role of the spiritual leader who for many centuries was a designated leader. Unlike in the early centuries, it was a role reserved for men. When one looks at Celtic Christianity in the seventh century, the structures there show a dual role for men and women. You had a woman leader like Saint Gobnait or, more importantly, the national saint, Saint Brigid of Kildare, as well as a Saint Kevin of Glendalough or a Saint Finbar of Gougane Barra. That dual role was certainly lost when the Normans brought a closer integration of a Christian practice with Rome. The Normans were a highly centralised civilisation, and they left far more of an imprint on government than say the Vikings had done for the two centuries before them. The Normans and the English both were government societies with a strong sense of centralisation. That influenced both Protestantism and Catholicism in Ireland in such a way that priest and bishop became an authoritative communicator and interpreter of spirituality for the people. And when one bears in mind that 90 per cent of the society continued to choose Roman Catholicism in the eighteenth and nineteenth centuries, it is not surprising that the priest became a central figure of power in the community. The priest's role in those centuries grew in significance also because very often he stood by his flock and was martyred together with it. There are still places in Ireland where flowers are put on the grave of a martyred priest: for example, in Cloheen in County Tipperary. I notice every time I visit the local graveyard, which is still in use, that there is always a fresh bunch of flowers on the grave of Father Sheehy, who was martyred not just for the faith, but also because he refused to break the seal of the confessional and identify for the military the local Whiteboys in the area. The Whiteboys were a secret agrarian society who administered a rough frontier justice on behalf of the oppressed. Here we have the association of a rebel priest identifying with his people, which we only see now in situations in South America from time to time.

These priests listened to their flock, they consoled the widows, they buried the dead. They also were Gaelic-speaking in Irish-speaking parts of the country, and they brought with them a great tradition which they might not even have been aware of, which actually went back beyond them to the monastic way of life which was intrinsic to the heroic period of Celtic

Christianity, and even further back, I would suggest, to the mysterious role of the pagan druid in Celtic society. Many cultural historians would see the priests of the eighteenth and nineteenth centuries as direct inheritors of the powers of the druid. It was not so much that he possessed magical powers or that he became the publicist of a code of ethics. In fact, perhaps these were totally missing. It was also probably true that the priest cohabited for all we know with a woman in the area: those things were not important in the eighteenth and nineteenth centuries. What was important was that in some way he was a carrier of an ancient spirituality which gave a subject people energy, and which connected too with the Celtic continuum.

The bonding between the modern and the ancient began to break up with the possibility of emigration to a new world: to Australia, to the Americas, and particularly to the United States. There you had a faith-bearing spiritual people suddenly precipitated into the slums of New York or Philadelphia or Boston, or into the prison camps of Australia. And the Irish priest followed them. In the penal settlements in the second half of the nineteenth century, invariably the Irish priest was present, and eventually then the convents of Irish sisters. All of them, I think, in some way were transmitters of the ancient Celtic spirituality, interlarded and, indeed, encased in a framework of devotions to the Sacred Heart, to Our Lady of Lourdes, to the Stations of the Cross, which sat easily upon the older... some call it faith, but I would say the older spirituality of these emigrant societies, a spirituality that was founded on the rock of a Celtic faith-world.

Coming back to the contemporary question: is that spirituality slipping away from the Irish people, now that the priest somehow has been dislocated in public perception, and sees himself losing touch with a past that was his lifeline? It is problematic. It is very hard to predict. I think it is going to be a very interesting test for Irish spirituality.

But the spirituality that interests me is a non-sacramental spirituality. I think Patrick Kavanagh brings it out very well in his poem called 'The Great Hunger'. It was a long poem written about the predicament of small farmers in the hungry 1940s, a period when the country stagnated. Europe was at war and Ireland seemed to be plunged into darkness. Kavanagh, who was, I think, our greatest poet of that mid-century, brought out powerfully in his poetry the frustration, the predicament, the uncomfortableness of the bachelor Irish farmer, poor, with no government incentives to improve his small forty- or thirty- or even fifteen-acre farm, to which he was tied. His sisters and brothers had gone off to America or to England, and he was left as the 'heir' to the farm, but also to take care of his widowed mother with whom he usually lived. Kavanagh brings out the longings, but also the spirituality of these small farmers. It is Kavanagh himself talking because he was in that situation before he decided to pull out of it and come to Dublin. There is one particular section where he goes through the seasons of the small farmer. This one is about March.

> The pull is on the traces, it is March
> And a cold black wind is blowing from Dundalk.
> The twisting sod rolls over on her back –
> The virgin screams before the irresistible sock.
> No worry on Maguire's mind this day
> Except that he forgot to bring his matches.
> 'Hop back there, Polly, hoy back, woa, wae,'
> From every second hill a neighbour watches
> With all the sharpened interest of rivalry.

Yet sometimes when the sun comes through a gap
These men know God the Father in a tree:
The Holy Spirit is the rising sap,
And Christ will be the green leaves that will come
At Easter from the sealed and guarded tomb.

I love the idea of the sun coming through a gap, because a gap between the fields in Ireland is usually a hostile gap. You don't go through gaps easily. You have to scrunch yourself through and avoid the nettles and avoid the thorns. And that kind of gap very often signifies territoriality, that you are passing from one farmer's field to another's, and yet we have Kavanagh's metaphor there of God the Father as a sun shining through such a hostile gap. These men know it, that is what Kavanagh is saying; these men realise it, that in the time of real famine or desperation, they will come together, they will forget rivalries and they will stand together on an issue, as they did with the land agitation.

I think that Kavanagh has caught the nature of our spirituality in that great poem. It is instinctive. It is almost pantheistic. But you can also see that intertwined with that sense of God is the catechism notion of God the Father, God the Son, Christ, and the Holy Spirit. This sense of the catechism, which was pounded into every school-going child; whatever about other subjects such as Irish, English or arithmetic, every child in the 1920s and the 1930s knew their catechism and knew the simple little instructions. Now, suppose that goes, that kind of dependence, if you like, which is a learned by rota, by memory, dependence on the Church, suppose that goes: will there then be the basic understructure of spirituality?

I believe there will. I believe that it is linked to family

memories, that the young generation of today will recall grand-parents who transcended the routine of the devotional, like saying the beads and going to daily mass. I think they also will remember those awkward moments in adolescence, or those poignant moments when a family sorrow draws a family together in bereavement, where an old person somehow will draw upon that vast reservoir of spirituality, and make sense of an action that is too deep for analysis.

I believe that my generation – we are now in our sixties – that we still are carriers of that older spirituality. And I think that many people in their sixties or seventies who are grand-aunts or grand-uncles or grandparents are not so much aware of a mission in any recognised sense, we are not imbued with a mission of passing on the heritage, but we have a sense of time pouring by and we are conscious of the fact that we transmit to the younger generation a sense of spiritual values, though they may no longer be linked with a cathecism or with a faith structure or with the Church and Church service.

I compare it myself to immigrants in places like Chicago from Russia or from Poland, who were insistent that their children certainly would modernise. For example, Polish families in Chicago disapproved if their children spoke Polish, and particu-larly the grandparents disapproved. The emphasis on speaking American-English was so important. It was an insistence on being American, but also, those same grandparents were the generation that gave their grandchildren a love of the values and the traditions of that part of Europe from which they came. So you have this curious mixture in American people who return to visit parts of Europe, that while they have lost the language, they have an amazingly deep interest in the folklife, in the stories, in the music of particular regions of Europe that they come from, and I would hope, and I would suspect, that in the present generation of older Irish people there is that sense of handing on something that we received with our mother's milk and took for granted. It was part of the cultural climate, it was part of the Church's ethos, it was part of the entertainment, it was part indeed of the Irish town.

Some of it is still there. When the Angelus rings out, people recognise it at twelve o'clock noon and at six o'clock. It is something that you take very much for granted. It is interesting that each time RTE has a debate on whether they should abandon the six o'clock Angelus, so many people write in and say, 'No, no, no, we want this to stay.' I think it reminds us of something special in our lives. When the bell rings, one is bound again to honour the spiritual within oneself. It is a reminder of another dimension to life rather than the one we are engaged on. People who might never think of saying the actual prayers of the Angelus yet like this icon appearing on the TV screen before the news at six o'clock. Maybe it sums up the ambivalence that we have concerning time, but also I think it symbolises an appreciation of a heritage that I would suspect Irish people on the whole do not wish to jettison with the coming of the information society. The information society takes its own toll too, you know; it taxes the human spirit. It really shuts down, if you like, on the whole quest for another world. It is so bounded by electronic messages that one loses a sense of mystery.

It is very good that people can switch off from the inexorable tick tock of the clock, the glancing at the wristwatch and the sense that time is measured out. To be able to stop that, to get off the assembly line and realise that we have all the time there is, which, when one thinks about it, is very profound: that actually the minute I stop breathing, I stop the time associated with myself. I am the author of my time. This is a dimension of spirituality that I think contemporary people are longing for in different forms, something that will bring them in touch with that suspension of activity that somehow will help them to enter into a timelessness. It is the seeking of the human spirit to find a plateau on which to rest. You may have to start climbing again, but for a little while you are on this plateau and you have a vision, just for a little while before you must go on.

This is really what I like about the rural spirituality which you find in remote parts of Ireland. These old fishermen and men and women that you meet along the secondary and the tertiary roads of Ireland, that you meet hanging over a bridge looking at other people doing the fishing, when you actually talk to them they have very often come to that sense of contentment which Kavanagh expresses time and again in his poetry.

People say about the Irish that they are drawn to suffering, and certainly when one looks at the past history of the people of this island, we have had our share of it. Into 1997, we will be honouring in a special way the whole disaster that famine can create in a society. We will go back to a subject that we didn't dare think about in my grandparents' time. What happened during the black years of 1846-48, when one million people died of hunger and one million fled the country carrying famine fever with them, and the population sank from eight million to four and a half within ten years, was a locked room in the memory. It was not thought about. A disaster like that, which is not spoken about maybe for two generations: the time comes when you have to take it out and honour it, and perhaps even mourn it, and also feel a bond with other societies which have recently endured or are enduring such a disaster.

We seem to be a memory-carrying people for sorrows. We can

go further back than the Famine of the mid-nineteenth century, and I suppose again one remembers the disaster of Cromwell's soldiers in a place like Drogheda, but when one sees the agony of wars in Africa or wars in central Europe, one is reminded that these are, sadly, the currencies of people's lives, that people can be contentedly living in an area little dreaming that war will sweep down, and then not just impersonal shells are coming from the air, but one's house, one's belongings, one's children and spouse will suddenly be taken away. Suffering like that can be an enduring resentment that will break out again in retaliation, but it can also somehow be reconciled with human experience through the memories handed down of shared experiences of how spirituality brought a people through an exile or through a disaster in time gone by. For example, in Ireland in the eighteenth century, when Roman Catholic services were forbidden by the state, the mass rock was hidden away in a lonely glen where a fugitive priest said mass for the local people and then went on his way. These are the kind of things that are maybe dropping out of memory now, but they won't ever quite drop out. There will always be somebody who will lead children to a place like that and say, 'Look, 300 years ago people came here in wet and cold and snow just to take the Eucharist and to break the bread of the Eucharist with each other.'

I see no easy definition of spirituality. In some ways I believe spirituality is the wrong word for it; that what we call spirituality is an exploration which is born in the inner self and carries out to the outer world. This kind of spirituality, and its connection with suffering, seems to me to be important to the human experience, because we cannot just shut out suffering from our lives, no matter how hard we try. It will impinge upon us eventually, and we will have to wrestle with it in a kind of solitary confusion. But when we, for example, embrace the suffering of a friend or relative, or when we share in a particular agony that a society endures, then it seems that our spiritual resources go beyond the self-centred quest for a meaning to 'my' life and have ramifications for the future of the whole planet.

Maureen Hogan

I WAS PLUCKING TURKEYS in Bantist when the first eye went. I used to give them a hand in the beginning when they got all these turkeys, and I said to Liam, my brother, that there must be a feather gone into my eye. He looked at it but couldn't see anything there. I feel it, I said, it is something soft, like a feather. He searched up and down but could still see nothing. Half of the vision was gone. I could see the top, but under that it was just a blur. So I went to the clinic in Nenagh. After a long time the doctor discovered this detached retina. When he did he sent me to Limerick where they operated. I had to stay for a month at the hospital.

After that the eye was okay for some time before it went again. The doctor said that I would have to go back to the hospital, but I didn't want to do that. It was an awful dose to lay down there on your back for a month. I wasn't really sick, you know. It was terrible, they had to feed me and I spilled tea on myself and got roasted. I didn't like it at all. I had one good eye and I thought that that was enough, and I had good sight in it. I thought that if you break one leg it is unlikely that you will break another one, so I didn't go back. Ten years later I lost the second eye and I knew better. I had taken Seamus, one of my sons, to the train in Thurles to go back to France. I had Tracey, my niece, with me in the car. I said to her on the way home that the day had gotten very dull. It wasn't that dull, she thought, but for me it was kind of hazy or something. That same

149

morning I had planned to go to the country market in Toomevara to deliver chickens, but I had to postpone that and go to the doctor instead. Maybe it was a sign of what was going to come, because on the way there I got a flat tyre. Two men must have seen me from a pub, because no sooner was the tyre empty than they were out helping me to fix it.

When the doctor saw my eye, he ordered an ambulance and sent me down to Cork. Beside me on the seat I had a man as good as dead. We had to stop in Mallow to put down a tube to get him breathing again. Then I lost my sight, and I never saw after that. It was like a black cloud came upon me. I don't really remember what I saw last. I remember seeing the college, Moorpark, on the way, but I can't remember if it was on that day I saw the boats on the River Lee or not. It is eleven years ago and I was very scared, very emotionally upset. I was crying terribly that day.

I didn't know what I was going to do when I came out first. I took it straight away that I wasn't going to have sight, and I didn't hold any hope for myself. I said I have to pull it up, to pull myself together and try and cope as best I can. I was very scared in the beginning. For example, I didn't dare to sit alone in a car if it was parked in an isolated parking space. They had to park somewhere in town where there were people around. I was afraid of my life. It didn't matter that it was in the middle of the day; in my eyes it was pitch dark. I am not afraid of that any more, but I am still afraid at night. If I hear a car stopping on the road, my heart starts beating faster, and as quick as lightning I will have my hand on the phone ready to call the Guards. So far, thank God, I haven't had to do it.

Being totally blind I didn't think I could manage in any way, but my daughter had come from Florida to bring me home from the hospital. One day she said that she would love a bit of the white soda bread that she had always liked so much, and asked me if I would try to bake it. 'It's impossible,' I said, but she insisted. 'Try it!' she said. So there you are. I tried it, and now I make cakes, tarts, Christmas cakes, the lot, ever since. After trying to make that bread, and succeeding, honest to God I never looked back. One needs that bit of an incentive, that bit of a shake. I said to myself that if I can do one thing I can do another, and when I could do another thing I could keep going. I actually had two rhubarb tarts made yesterday, but I had visitors in the evening and when I came to the kitchen this morning I couldn't find the smallest bit, so I had to make another tart this morning. But you know, I wouldn't be able to make a tart or anything if you or somebody else were here chatting. See, I can only do it when I have no distractions. If not, I lose concentration and forget what ingredients I have already put in, and I can't look and see what I have missed. Usually the result is quite good. I didn't see it as a particularly big achievement if something turned out nice for me before I got blind, but I do now. Now I think it is a compliment to myself. Queen cakes are my biggest problem. I can make the pastry all right, but I can't get them into the paper forms. They always tip over. I don't know what to do, but there must be a way.

I have a big preparation to do for the next two weeks. I am having twenty-five members of the ICA, the Irish Countrywomen's Association, of which I am a member, coming to a party. We have a meeting every month, and every month there are two hostesses who bring tea, cakes, and we have a little party, you see, after the meeting, a little tea and a chat. That is something I can't do. I couldn't make sandwiches and share them out. I wouldn't know where the tables were or anything. So to recompense for all that I bring them to the house once a year. The only difference is basically that the meeting is in my home instead of at the hall. It might be a little bit extra. The women say it is like coming to a hotel.

I am going to cook almost every single little bit myself. I will have to start very soon to get everything ready in time, as I am a bit slower now. I actually have a cake made already, I just have to put icing on it, and then I will have two fruit-cakes, heavy ones, with rum and lots of fruit in. I find rum gives the best flavour. Then I will make four light fruit-cakes with just a little bit of fruit, not much. I cook them in an hour. The heavy ones take three and a half hours. I will make two tarts, possibly one raspberry and one apple, and I am cooking a leg of ham, deboned. The ham is going to be served with potato salad. I don't make the potato salad myself, though. One of the family will do that. I am not a salad eater, so I wouldn't be good at it. But I will cook everything else that needs to be cooked and have everything prepared. Then, there I stop. I can't dish them out.

Philomena, my other brother's wife, and another Country-woman from the Templederry branch, will come down to help me with it. I will have everything there for them. I tell them what to do then. I get plates – now, breakfast-plates, not the big dinner-plates – and I get them to put two nice slices of meat, a spoonful of potato salad and possibly half a tomato and a leaf of lettuce on each, and a slice of brown, a slice of white and a slice of loaf, and hand them around to each of the women with a knife and fork. Then, when that is finished they will have other plates ready with a bit of fruit cake and tart. And whenever that is over they get a bit of a dessert. I will probably have strawber-ries and jelly and cream.

As I said, in the beginning I didn't know what to do with myself. I didn't want to go out. I was so scared of getting lost.

Today I am cool when anything goes wrong. I don't panic any more. I often get lost in the yard but I usually keep walking until I find my way. People don't notice it when they have their sight, but if you walk on a little stone your foot will turn, and you will take another direction. When you see you don't think about it because you correct it automatically, but I can't do that, and when I realise that I am lost, then it is already too late to run back. When people say to me to keep walking straight it doesn't mean anything to me. I can't walk straight. If I have to walk without help over an open space, I am lost and I can end up anywhere.

Last year I wanted to go to the field beside the house to get some potatoes. Instead of that I got completely lost. I couldn't get out of it. Sometimes I have a phone in a bag around my neck when I go out for a longer walk, say up to the cross or so, in case I would need somebody's help, but not this time. I wouldn't carry it with me around the yard anyway. Now, I was a little bit scared to walk around on the field too much, because I knew there was a drain there and I was scared I would fall down into it. I kept listening and listening. There aren't many cars coming on this road, but when I heard the milk-lorry I faced the way it was coming and tried to locate myself that way, but without success.

I had a bucket with me. I turned it upside down and paused on it. By now I had spent a couple of hours out there – and what the heck did I hear eventually, didn't the cock crow? God, I said, I wish it would crow again, 'cause I knew he spent all his time under the apple-trees waiting for an apple to fall, and he did. He gave another crow and I moved a couple of steps in his direction and – I hit the wire! I couldn't believe it. I was so close, and at the same time so far away that I might as well have been in Timbuktu.

I didn't like being lost, of course not; it is always a bit scary, but I was still pretty satisfied with this particular day. You see, when I was resting on the bucket I started to feel a bit hungry, and suddenly I realised how I would manage to fry a sausage! It is easy to fry a chop or a T-bone steak or anything like that, it is only to turn them around, but how do you turn around a sausage? I suddenly got the idea that I could split them in the middle, lengthwise. Not a big discovery for mankind, I know, but for me it solved a problem and gave me a tiny bit more of independence.

You have to fight against yourself, because it is so easy to sit down and say: 'Would you ever give me a cup of tea? Would you ever get me a slice of bread? Could you please do this or that for me?' If you get into your head in the beginning that you can't even get up and make a cup of tea, that it is not possible to do it, then you won't even try to do it. I know, there are lots of times when it is tough going, lots of times. They say that you will accept your blindness, but that is not true. You can't get used to it and you can't accept it. All you can do is to keep going. We just have to take the bad days with the good days and always be prepared for losses, and however big the losses have been for me, I wouldn't change a thing in my life. Ups and downs, deaths and sickness, I would still carry on. I reckon it was an act of God, a little bit of punishment, and then, maybe I have seen enough. Maybe He doesn't want me to see a lot of the things that are happening today? But whatever the reason is, I haven't made that many changes since I lost my sight. At least I don't think so. I'm just a normal housewife. I do everything as far as possible that I did all the time. I was milking the cow up to a few years ago, and I reared her calves. I had a guideline that I followed over the yard to the cowhouse, and as soon as I opened the door to it, she would come from wherever she was. She just gave an odd cough to tell she was on the way. She was usually laying down by the river. I would have another cow today if I only could train her, although I would be a bit scared that she would push me over. I am getting a bit old, you know.

Yes, I do my own share around the yard. I have, I don't know exactly how many, but I suppose it would be about fifty hens that I take care of, and collect and sell the eggs from. I know where they lay most of the eggs so it is not that difficult to find them. There is only an odd nest that I miss. It has happened too that a clucking hen has come from some corner with half a dozen or a dozen chirping chickens around her. But I know roughly how many hens I have by counting the eggs.

I take care of the heating of the house myself, like I always did. Whenever I need I go to the turf-house and fill up my four-stone bag and bring it in and put it in the box. I bought a lorry of turf on Monday but I don't know if it is good, though. I hope it is, because I paid £79 for it. Did you see it when you came in? Does it look black enough? Good turf should be hard and black-ish, the blacker the better. The turf is said to be terrific this year. I like to have a good fire going when I sit down in the evening to write a letter or to listen to the radio or to knit.

When I am saying I do my share around the yard, I mean it. I couldn't do everything, of course not. I couldn't, for example, manage the cattle or the fields. John, my youngest son, comes down every weekend from Dublin and takes care of that. We have about fifty-five acres of land and every bit of it is good land. The soil is very deep.

The only thing that really kills me is that I am not indepen-dent. To a point I am, but let nobody tell you 'Oh, Maureen Hogan, she is so independent,' because that is not right. I can't

155

drive the car for one thing and that I miss more than anything. You see, when I had my sight I would be really quick after having baked the bread or got the lads out to school. I would get into the car real fast and visit some of my friends over around Cloughjordan for an hour. I loved meeting people, and I still do. It wasn't every day, but when I wanted to go I did. Today, if I want to go somewhere, I need to have somebody with me. Before, if I wanted fruit from down the country, I could just take my car and go and nobody would know where I was. It was really private. I could tip into town and do whatever I wanted as long as I was back to get the dinner ready for the kids when they came home from school. It was a great freedom. I used to go to the country market once a week with tarts, bread, chicken, cabbage and rhubarbs. I often got up at six o'clock in the morning and cut a hundred dozen stalks of rhubarb. O'Connor alone would take fifty or sixty dozen twice a week. Sure there wasn't much money in it, but every penny counted and they cost nothing to grow anyway.

Sometimes my husband would help me, but he wasn't always healthy and spent periods of time in bed. He is dead now for over twenty years.

Yes, I lost the eyes and I lost the car, but I won the bird-song. Before I lost my sight I was too busy to listen to the birds. I was always running around doing something. Now I have peace and calm and it is so beautiful in the spring mornings when the birds start singing. Then I know it is dawn.

Also from Brandon

Chet Raymo
Honey from Stone

In a series of lyrical meditations on science, nature and religion, physics professor Chet Raymo ponders the relevance of traditional belief in a world described by contemporary science.

'An entrancing meditation on stones and stars and mossy ruins... Raymo revels in the mysteries explored by science.'
San Francisco Chronicle

'Precisely lyrical, deeply prayerful despite metaphysical scepticism, this is the work of one who, besides being a science professor, is a true poet.' *Publishers Weekly*

'Lovely essays brimming with nature mysticism... Raymo begins by wondering what value the traditional religion of his childhood holds in the contemporary scientific cosmos. He concludes by hedging his bets... yet he revels in religious imagery, using it to accentuate his sense of wonder at the mysteries of the natural world.' *Kirkus Review*

'*Honey from Stone* is... a travel book about the world of ideas. Raymo uses the natural setting of Dingle as a place in which he asks you to explore with him through his own private universe... *Honey from Stone* is a beautiful book that is well worth reading.'
Irish Echo

ISBN 0 86322 232 3; 160 pages; £6.99 pb

Stephen Rynne
Green Fields: A Journal of Irish Country Life

No one wrote about the farming life with as much insight as Stephen Rynne. From the naming of cattle to the choice of seed potatoes and apples, the details of rural life are recorded with the true countryman's eye, with humour and affection but without sentimentality.

'There is no excuse for not possessing one of the great personal chronicles of the modern Irish countryside. It is a book one falls deeply in love with.' *Irish Times*

'This 1938 gem deserves to share a category with Joyce.'
Books Ireland

'A most welcome reprint of a little classic.'
Ireland of the Welcomes

ISBN 0 86322 203 X; 252 pages; £7.95 pb

Rebecca Millane
The Gift Healers

This book offers a portrait of healers, ordinary men and women who possess a precious gift of healing. They achieve regular, sometimes remarkable success in restoring their patients' health. While some use herbs, the main element of their healing is a gift, beyond scientific understanding.

'Her lively journalistic style and fine storytelling has made *The Gift Healers* not only a very interesting and informative book but a very readable one into the bargain.' *Tuam Herald*

0 86322 210 2; 117 pages; £7.95 pb